Alan D

CW00820987

A Tour-Guide's Life

A short history of Tourism and its possible future...

Second and revised edition

Other books by Alan DeMaze

France and the French, a journey from the Carthaginians to Napoleon III   (third edition)

Spain, Portugal, and the Iberians

The Germans, from Marius to Bismarck

The Cosmic Surfer, a short guide to surviving the 21st century… and beyond

A Surfer's guide to Sunshine and Rainbows

The Journey and the Destination

The Tide is up

Foreword

In the wake of the coronavirus pandemic and the devastating consequences it might have on the global economy, I thought to revise this small essay.

As it happens, in times of crisis, tourism is always one of the first industries to suffer. Until now, it had always managed to recover. This time though, it might become the victim of an inexorable snowball effect...

Since the late 1960's, early 1970's, mass-travel has enjoyed an ever increasing success, but it didn't go without changes. In fact, major transformations have taken place in the last few years. Air-and-land touring, fly-and-drive lost a lot of its charm under the repeated assaults of the cruise industry, and in particular, the low-cost cruises, cheap and cheerful "club-med", on the rivers and on the seas...

Right from the start of the pandemic, these leisure floating villages, which for some had become cities of nearly 10,000 guests and staff, proved vulnerable health wise. As a result, their future has become most uncertain.

These relatively inexpensive vacations had recently become most popular. Indeed, they were just about the only ones many people could afford. Better even, thanks to their historical background, cruises

1

had an aura of ultimate comfort and elegance which most passengers never thought they could afford, budget classy vacations, inexpensive luxury! A very incongruous concept indeed, and it sold!

Well, this might be over. Social distancing and other necessary health measures will make such vacations very complicated to run. In turn, they will be much more expensive for the customers to purchase, and not just the cruises either, but also the bus tours. It will be very much the same in hotels and restaurants, in museums and other popular tourist sites, as well as on airplanes of course.

Although, by fear of going out of business, some operators would rather ignore the issue and restart their activity as if nothing had happened, things have changed.

Many people think this will pass, like everything else, but the first contamination cases which will inevitably occur, on a ship, on a bus, on a plane, or in a restaurant, will reinforce the doubts some may have, and clearly, anxiety is not what people are looking for when they book a vacation.

Ultimately, this will lead to a general disaffection for low-cost mass travel. It may soon appear as a relic of the past, as something people used to do for leisure at least once in their life in the olden days.

In turn, and this is the most dramatic part, the downfall of mass travel might simply reshape the world economy... the snowball effect...

Around the age of six, after reading Daniel Defoe's "Robinson Crusoe", I started drawing sail boats. By the time I finished "Around the World in 80 Days", by Jules Verne, I had caught the travel-bug!

I went to boarding school when I was eight, and travelling associated with dreaming, escaping, and ultimately, with vacations. Between you and me, I was not too happy to be locked up in a classroom! However, when the vacations came, we'd go places with the parents. We'd get on the car and change the daily horizon: different sights, different people, different noises, different smells, and even different languages... When the parents got divorced, it became more complicated...

In the summer of 1967, I was fourteen; my mother took me to Italy. It was my first trip abroad, and from then on, every year, I went to some country or other.

So, we went to Decenzano, on Lake Garda, for two weeks. The place was great. Every day, I spent hours swimming in the blue waters of the lake. Then, two or three times a week, we went on excursions. Our host, nowadays we'd call him the local rep, was a most charming man. Monsieur Landier was his name. He was very knowledgeable, indeed a local expert. He took us on these side trips that make any holiday memorable.

The full day excursion to Venice was one of the best. After the glassblowing demonstration at a venue near Saint Mark's Square, we had some free time, to do some window-shopping for some, to enjoy a drink at one of the famous sidewalk cafés for a few others, or more simply, to visit Saint Mark's Basilica and the Doges' Palace, rarely ever crowded in those days.

After a brief visit to the Basilica, I went to the Doges' Palace which I visited on my own. I was so impressed that I started writing an essay when I went back to school, a few weeks later. I never had the chance to finish it though…

On another day, we visited the villa of a famous Italian poet and national hero, Gabriele D'Annunzio, in Gardone Riviera. He was somewhat of a wealthy eccentric: on top of a biplane, he owned a midget submarine which was on display in the garden!

Of course, we did the usual drive along the narrow winding mountain roads of the Dolomites, spectacular…

My mother must have thought I was a little too energetic. The following summer, in 1968, she sent me to Essen, Germany, with a bunch of other high school kids. We stayed with local families.

Language class in the morning, excursions in the afternoon... I quickly skipped the excursions; spending time with the locals was much more fun!

The following year, I went to England. I stayed with a great family in Farnborough, Hants, Mr. and Mrs. Bush. I had told my mom, no language class, no excursions! When I ran out of pocket money, after a couple of weeks, Mr. Bush offered me a job... I made 5£ a week, great money in those days! Spending time with him and his co-workers was a lot of fun and great language practice. Then, on weekends, I used to go to London to play tourist! This was definitely a lot of fun...

In 1970, after my motorbike accident, my mom took me to Spain, beach vacation in Gandia, near Valencia: my two favorite ingredients, sea and sun!

In 1971, I spent five weeks in Germany making some pocket money working in a small town near Stuttgart, great language practice. Then I went to Formentera, the smallest of the Balearic Islands: two or three weeks of sea and sun!

As the island was undeveloped at the time, just a few rare houses here and there, tucked among the pines and nothing on the waterfront, I slept on the beach with a few other people. Late morning every day, this local guy arrived with his small fishing boat. He prepared the best grilled fresh fish, the catch of the day, at the greatest price! It was a heavenly vacation away from civilization! No electricity, nothing, just sand, sea, and sun!

Then, the following year, when I got out of high school, I went on a very long trip. I hitchhiked around Europe for over two months, nearly three. I went as far as Vienna, Austria, then down to Yugoslavia, all the way to Dubrovnik. There was no easy way from there to Greece, but thanks to my student ID card, I was able to get on a cheap flight to Athens, on an old DC-4.

I stayed at the cheapest hotel in town, the "Sans Rival", on the roof, with a bunch of other backpackers. Then I took a boat to Rhodes. I slept on the deck where I ran into a bunch of people with whom I traveled for a while. After a few days in Rhodes, visiting Lindos and a few other sites, we crossed to Marmaris, on the Turkish side. There, we caught a bus to Istanbul, the gateway to the Orient, the old Silk Road…

When the others returned home, I went back to Rhodes and from there to Mykonos. "Super-Paradise Beach" was the place to go to at the time, no disco, no fancy restaurant, just a bunch of sun seekers, mostly from the States. We looked like a colony of seals and sea lions lazing on the beach!

Then I headed for Crete. Once again, I met other backpackers with whom I traveled around the island, Matala, Heraklion, Agios Nikolaos, catching the sights of the old Minoan civilization as we went along, in Knossos and other parts.

When the time came to go north again, I caught a boat from Piraeus to Venice, through the Corinth Canal, deck-class as always, but what a ride! Then I hitch-hiked my way to Marseille, to visit some friends, and finally, I headed for Aix-en-Provence for a few days. Funny enough, on the first day, as I strolled along the streets, catching the atmosphere, I ran into my mother's friend. He invited me for dinner, the first real meal in a while!

I was back in Paris some time end of September. I went to art school… It was fall, then winter. It was grey, dark grey, and it was not funny.

In February, I thought to go to Ibiza and from there to Formentera, but there were very few boats out of Barcelona, too scarce and too expensive so, I ended up going to Corsica instead, for a week! It was too cold to swim, but the sun felt great!

One evening, in May, as she got home from work, my mom said to me, "Alan, why don't you get a summer job?" Great idea!

The next day, I was running around Paris looking for… a summer job. The man at Manpower said, "Drop by any morning at five, we'll have a job for you." Naively, I asked if he had anything where I could use my languages, English and German. He smiled and kindly suggested I apply with the Travel Agencies. I had no idea what or where… He said I'd find them along the Rue de Rivoli, across the street from the Louvre Museum and the Tuileries Gardens.

Off I was, my hair down on my shoulders, my old bleached blue jeans and my favorite tennis shoes on, with a light white cotton embroidered shirt I'd brought back from Istanbul, the peace and love days, and a black corduroy jacket on top of it all, the perfect art student outfit, nothing fancy to say the least!

I missed the first travel agency, "Rapid Pullman", next to the Regina Hotel and the statue Joan of Arc, on the Pyramid Square. The second one, "Cityrama", was a bit further down, tucked away in a small side street. I missed it too! I was walking along the third and last one, "France Tourisme-Paris Vision", when I looked up and realized it must have been what I was looking for.

I walked to the counter, "Hello, I speak English and German and I'm looking for a summer job." The lady behind the counter, Françoise was most gracious. She smiled and said, "Oh, you have to speak with Monsieur Peter." Hearing his name, Monsieur Peter looked up and walked from the back of the office to shake my hand.

After we sat down, he started speaking to me in German. He was from somewhere near Frankfurt, and whatever he said sounded totally alien. My German was like my jeans, very faded, to say the least! As a matter of fact, my English was almost as bad. Nevertheless, he told me to come back the following week, with a proper jacket and a tie. "A tie?" I nearly died!

I wasted no time. I was there the following Monday. I wore my only jacket, a winter jacket, most uncomfortable. We were in May, 1973, and it was abnormally warm. My one and only tie was killing me, not to mention my one and only buttoned shirt; it was kind of old and it felt one size too small!

After a few evenings of training on Paris-by-Night tours, illuminations, Seine cruise, and the cabarets, the Lido and the Moulin Rouge, I spent the Friday evening with some friends, celebrating someone's birthday. We finished at two in the morning in a busy café in the Latin Quarter, on the Left Bank. The people who sat next to us walked away, and, talk about a coincidence, the assistant manager of the travel agency where I'd spent the week training came and sat at the empty table with his wife. "Hey, Alan, we'll be busy tomorrow. Come in early, you'll be working!"

That was the start of a long ride on a heck of a rollercoaster!

Later on, I learned that my boss at France Tourisme, Monsieur Peter had been expecting the friend of a friend of his, apparently also named Alan, and he had mistaken me for whoever this guy was! I guess I was lucky!

In any case, Monsieur Peter had previously worked as a tour-guide for a well known European Tour Operator with American groups. He had these black and white pictures on the wall of his office which arouse my curiosity...

On one of the very first evenings that I worked as a night-guide, around mid-June, as we were taking the clients back to their hotels after the show at the Moulin Rouge, our bus got stuck on a narrow street. Cars were parked on both sides, and one in particular was closer to the middle of the street. While the bus driver and I were trying to lift it out of the way, I guess it was a small car, most clients got off and left.

This lady from California who travelled with her son and two daughters stayed until we were done. Sometime later, I received a letter from her. Val was her name. She kindly invited me to come and visit her and her family in Carmel, California, if I ever was in the States...

At the time, it seemed highly unlikely, but I wrote back thanking her, and I kept her letter.

Shortly after, I quit the night-guide thing. The same illuminations, boat ride and cabaret every night was an extremely well paid job for a twenty year old art student, but it was totally boring! So, I tried my luck with other things. I needed a bit of a challenge!

I eventually started working as an assistant sales manager for a small wholesale chemical company, but, in the aftermath of the 1973 oil crisis, business was bad. After about a year, a little more, they let me go, with a more than respectable financial compensation...

I could have looked for some other similar job and settled in some kind of routine, but adventure sounded a lot more fun! This unexpected sum of money was the one chance that I had to ever travel to the US.

Thanks to my first job as a night-guide, I had a few friends in the business. It always helps! This ex-colleague of mine worked at the American Legion in Paris. At the time, charter flights were not available in France, but through her, I was able to get a cheap flight out of Brussels to New York. I landed there at the beginning of December, 1975.

A transfer was included in the deal, from JFK to downtown Manhattan. While we drove past all these graveyards, this guy on the microphone was telling us about the McAlpin hotel, on 34th and Broadway, across the street from Macy's. He also mentioned the driveaway car companies as an inexpensive way to travel around the States. I ended up staying a few days at the McAlpin, for $10 a night, back in the day, and I found myself a car heading west.

At first, they offered me to take a Corvette down to Albuquerque, New Mexico. At the time, I had no idea what a Corvette was, but New Mexico sounded a bit out of the way. So, I ended up with an Eldorado 1973, which I had to take to Chicago…

That's right, the cars they offered me had some of the worst gas mileage! Not such a good deal after all to say the least, but the driving was fun and really comfortable!

The Eldorado was impressive, white, with a white leather interior, V8, 800 horsepower engine, yes, 800, like a formula one monster in those days! It was more powerful than most 5O seater tour buses in Europe!

So, off I was! I had never driven such a huge car in my life, but I got used to it. When I tried to push the engine, to see how fast it could go, I got myself a $25 ticket for speeding! Oh, well...

I was on my way to Saint Louis, to visit this lady I had met on the plane. Her father, Ted Flax, lived on Bardot Lane, easy to remember for a Brigitte Bardot fan! I eventually found the place, and the next morning, I was off to Chicago. As I got there in the middle of the night, I went to sleep in the back of the car, until I could deliver it first thing the next morning.

Windy City was cold. It started snowing that day! So, I got another car, another Cadillac, a four door Sedan de Ville, same year, 1973, just bigger than the Eldorado. It was huge! By then though, I was used to the craft. It went to San Francisco, just what I needed.

First, I drove down to Saint Louis again, and the next morning, I headed due west. It was pretty straightforward. As I slept on the back seat, I was able to do very good timing. As a result, I was three or four days ahead of schedule and so, I decided to make a detour via Carmel. I wanted to check on this lady and her family whom I had met three years before on my Paris-by-night tour. I arrived in Carmel late afternoon, early evening on Friday, and I found an inexpensive motel.

The hot shower felt great! Then I called my friends. They were surprised to hear that I was down the road! One of the two daughters, Lisa was on her way to meet me. I think we went out for a bite. I was starving. I had to eat something! I met the rest of the family the following day.

I stayed with them for a few days, in this small cabin, next to the main house. It was great, but I had to deliver the car in San Francisco where I spent a week at the Grant Hotel. Then, I had to get to L.A. where I was supposed to meet this guy. He had offered me to model for his bathing suits collection, except that by the time I got there, it was too late, he was already done.

However, he suggested that I get in touch with this man who told me I should come for dinner at his place. When I said I would gladly meet him for lunch, and definitely not at his home but in a restaurant, he had this loud and mocking laugh, very loud, and very mocking indeed... And yes, before it even started, it was the end of my modeling career! Oh, well...

So, I got in touch with this other guy, Lionel. He was a friend of my former boss in Paris, Monsieur Peter. He worked at the L.A. office of the Tour Operator Peter had worked for in the past as a tour-guide.

When I told him about my modeling adventures, he laughed. He said I should write to his European headquarters and apply for a job, which I did. By the time I got back to Paris, late March, early April, I had a letter inviting me on a training tour.

Monsieur Peter suggested I get in touch with their Paris manager, Sigi, a Bavarian, a great guy. He told me to call Mr. so and so, one of the managers of the company in Switzerland, and ask him to put me on the first training tour instead of the second one on which I was booked... He laughed, but it worked!

And I got lucky once again! Out of over eighty applicants, we had two buses, nearly full, only seventeen or eighteen were hired and I was one of them, very proud indeed!

A few of us spent an extra day playing tourists on the Swiss lake, and off I was, overnight train back to Paris, home sweet home...

A couple of weeks later, I received my first allocation, a three week tour of Europe, going all the way down south to Athens and flying back to London. I was over the moon!

Although I was totally broke, the thought of working and making money had nothing to do with my being ecstatic. I was going to travel, even better, I was actually going to be paid to travel, and for me, traveling has always been synonymous with having fun!

Enjoying what I do is the key to being happy!

My first tour started in Paris. They flew in from New York with Capitol Airways, a charter company. For practical reasons, all the economy groups that flew in with Capitol stayed at the same hotel, a big tower on the east side of Paris, within easy reach of the airport.

I was lucky. My driver, a Dutchman by the name of Bram knew every corner of every street in Europe. All I had to do was go around the bus, smile and do some PR, with a few comments once in a while. In the bigger cities, Bram whispered me the info. Yes, he made the tour! In those days, a good driver was essential to do a good tour.

We went parallel with three or four other groups which we lost in Rome. They headed north again, while we continued south, towards Naples, Capri, and Sorrento. The next day, on to Brindisi, to cross over to Greece, my favorite part of the trip! We stayed at a fabulous hotel in Athens, the Grande Bretagne, with a huge pool on the roof, a dream! Then we flew to London for the last two nights, nothing out of the ordinary.

On the other hand, my second tour was… out of the ordinary, totally so indeed! Forty five days! One and a half months, with the same people, going all over the place, nearly!

This is where the challenge really started!

You might have seen this movie, "*If it's Tuesday, this must be Belgium*". It's a 1969 Hollywood production, and a fairly accurate depiction of what a European bus tour was like in those days, something truly hilarious, an enormous amount of fun, both, the tours and the movie!

Things have changed since then, drastically so, and in many ways… The good old days, as it says, the good old days. We have unfortunately lost the poetry. Oh, well…

There is also the brilliant 1964, John Huston's rendition of "*The Night of the Iguana*", a masterpiece, although on a slightly different note, but still.

Watch them both if you haven't yet, or watch them again if you already have!

So anyway, my forty five days traveling experiment started in London, one of my favorite cities since the first time I was there, back in 1969.

The morning after the arrival of the group, the day began with the guided city-tour which ended at Buckingham Palace with the Change of the Guard. Then, some must have gone to Stratford-upon-Avon, in search of some Shakespearian inspiration; others went shopping of course!

Evenings were free. Not only did they speak the language, but I'd had an awfully bad experience on my very first tour. On the last evening, I had offered an optional Dinner and Show excursion which had nearly turned into a disaster.

The coach, an old Bedford that was supposed to take us from the restaurant near Oxford Circus at the top of Regent Street down to the Palladium to attend a concert by Julie Andrews broke down on the way. We were all dressed up, the ladies had their heels on, and we'd had to run to get to the theatre on time. To make things worse, it was hot; we had a heat wave! This nerve-racking experience had most definitely been the one too many. I never offered an optional excursion in London again, ever, day or night!

Apart from this one-and-only near catastrophe, London was always fun and trouble free, thanks to the language of course. If they got lost on the underground, they could always ask for directions…

On the other hand, once we got to the continent, it was a totally different ballgame. There, they depended entirely on us, tour-guides, for assistance.

After being spoiled on my very first tour with Bram, my Dutch driver who knew Europe like the back of his hand, Peppe, a very nice man from Madrid, Spain, was a total novice north of the Pyrenees. Don't get me wrong, he was a very experienced driver, but he only did tours in Spain and Portugal, sometimes venturing into Morocco…

As soon as we met in Calais, we started a long series of getting lost! We didn't have GPS in those days, just the good old unfolding paper maps. On a 45 day tour going all over the place, you would need a whole suitcase of them, national and local, as well as a bunch of detailed city maps. In fact, some of my colleagues carried an extra attaché case just for them. On top of the set of maps being very costly, their attaché case was extremely heavy!

In any case, as I was broke, I mean really broke, I couldn't afford either the maps or the attaché case, bottom line! Apart from my old unfolding European roadmap, which I'd used some years before to hitchhike around Europe, all the way to Vienna, Istanbul, and back, I didn't have any, nor did Peppe for that matter! He had trusted that I would know my way around, and I had expected him to be a road expert like my first driver!

The very first day on the continent, we went from Calais to Paris, for three nights. We stayed at this western suburb hotel, the Penta. I knew it well, but we missed it! Bad omen! It was easy enough to drive around the block though, and we sorted that out in no time.

Although I was home, it was only my second time in Paris with a tour group! I had to change perspective. I had to think bigger picture. It was not an evening out with a few people and then bye-bye, like when I was a night-guide back in 1973. It was a tour, a whole tour, and this one was a very long one indeed. I had to think long term, different concept. Yes, I had to learn, and if the 45 day proved a total financial disaster, at least it was a great training tour! If I survived it, I could do anything!

On the first evening, I offered an optional dinner in Montmartre, followed by a drive around illuminated Paris, the city of lights. As a trained Paris-by-night guide, it was my specialty! The next day started with the included morning city-tour, followed by an afternoon optional trip to Versailles. In the evening, I took them to the Moulin Rouge. The following day was at leisure. They had time to go to the Louvre. Some went window shopping I guess…

After Paris, we headed for Brussels, a one night stop at the Palace Hotel, right in the center, easy to find.

Then we went to Amsterdam, a two night stop. Our hotel, the Arthur Frommer was way out of town, near the airport. I had been there on my first tour. I knew it was difficult to get to, but I trusted my luck…

As we were getting closer, I told the group that the ground floor was below sea-level. We could actually see the hotel, right there, on the left side of the bus. I will never forget the sight…

It had been a great summer day. The sky was immaculate blue, and the sun, a huge orange ball was setting on the horizon, right behind the hotel…

Well, we missed the exit! The Arthur Frommer was next to this highway interchange, and if you didn't pay attention, you had to drive around for a while, and that's exactly what we did… We eventually got there. I must have found some silly excuse or another, in the hope of getting away with it…

The sightseeing tour the next day included a canal cruise, then I offered an excursion to Marken and Volendam, on the Markermeer Lake, just north of Amsterdam, nice and laid back in those days.

Dinner at the hotel, and early morning departure the following day.

I have no recollection of the Hamburg hotel. Clearly, it was not the highlight of the tour!

We had a Tour Escort from Hawaii in the group, a former military, whatever his name was, Rick, or Bob, or something of the kind. He travelled with a small group of eight or ten people. He had been all over the place several times before, and he was well aware of the local Red Light District of Hamburg known as the *Reeperbahn*. We must have been too far out of town in Amsterdam for him to go to the local bars, downtown, so, in Hamburg, he asked me to organize an evening excursion to one of the shows.

After dinner, on the first evening, he and I took a taxi to this place where they offered me a deal. The next night, about half of the group came along, after I warned them very strongly and explicitly about the nature of the show.

Maybe some didn't quite catch what I tried to explain. A few of them left during the first half! Neither they nor the others who stayed until the end ever said a word. Clearly though, it was not a place to go back to!

Next morning, departure for Copenhagen, Denmark. Upon arrival, the usual hesitations to reach the SAS Hotel, worsened by the inevitable summer roadworks which became my main excuse for the daily detours! Yes, they were a very patient group!

The Little Mermaid was there, on our guided morning city-tour. Then, most of them went to some castle, on the afternoon optional extension.

Berlin was the next destination, West Berlin.

After a quick overnight ferry crossing, we landed at Warnemünde, in Russian controlled East Germany, the land of the ultimate enemy for most Americans at the time. Not a whisper… They clearly were in a hurry to reach the free world again! Yes, it was a relief to get to our hotel that night.

The next day, the city-tour was followed by an excursion to the Pergamom Museum, on the east side. Crossing Checkpoint Charlie was definitely one of the highlights of the tour! The security on both sides, west and east, was so incredible, it made the experience more thrilling than a spy movie! Everyone had a huge rush of adrenaline!

We got another local guide on the other side. She was an expert of the area, and she spoke perfect English. They had a ball! The East was not so bad after all! We crossed Checkpoint Charlie again, back to the West. When we got back to the hotel, everyone enjoyed a *weiße* mit schuss, the local specialty, a Berlin white beer poured over a shot of raspberry liquor or just about anything sweet as per your taste, very palatable and refreshing on a hot summer day!

The next day, we crossed into East Germany again. We traveled on the historical freeway built before WWII to connect Berlin with Munich, the very first *Autobahn*!

It was in the same shape as at the end of the war. It had never been repaired. It was full of holes and bumpy, but it did the trick, it got us to the west! The lunch stop was at a road side restaurant, and so was the coffee break in the afternoon, not much for comfort in those days… but as it says, when you've got to go, you've got to go!

Everyone was relieved when we reached the border, and even more so when we got to our charming family owned hotel in Rothenburg ob der Tauber, on the Romantic Road.

It was a brilliant place, right on the old medieval wall… until they served dinner. *Leberwurst Suppe* was on the menu, soup of pork liver sausage, a local specialty…

"Alan, what is it we're eating?" I can still hear the tone of voice and the Brooklyn accent! That was the end of that! "OK guys, let's go for beer and pretzels at the next-door *Bierfest*, on me!" It saved the situation! I got reimbursed of course, and it earned me the compliments of my boss! I believe they changed the menu for the next group!

The next morning, we left the joyous atmosphere of the summer beer gardens of Germany and headed for the Rhine Falls, always spectacular. Then, across the Black Forest, the land of Cuckoo Clocks and dark chocolate and wild cherries sponge cake, we carried on to Switzerland, the land of luxury watches and crunchy chocolate, hmmm…

The next day was busy: after a brief orientation tour of Lucerne, we took a trip up Mount Pilatus. After the unavoidable shopping, mostly window-shopping that is, we had an optional Cheese Fondue and Swiss Folklore evening at a local venue, with the Alpenhorn and the yodeling. A picture perfect tourist day in Lucerne, Switzerland!

By then, just over two weeks after the start of the tour in London, they were already getting tight on budget! Some might have had a bar of chocolate, black, white, or milk chocolate, plain, or with raisins or nuts, but no flashy famous watch brand at their wrist!

There was one more month to go, yes, one more whole month!

From Lucerne, the itinerary is straightforward... Lichtenstein for the morning coffee break, and lunch at the Café Pfanne, one of the roadside restaurants at Saint Anton on the Arlberg Pass, (nowadays there's a tunnel). They had a fabulous apple strudel, with tons of whipped cream of course!

Then, on to Innsbruck... In those days, it was still a quiet little town. It was just before the 1976 Winter Olympics. Orientation tour on arrival, a bit of free time to loosen up those stiff legs, and then, after dinner, the Tyrolean Folk Show at the local brewery. The next morning, on to Vienna, via Salzburg.

For many people at the time, Salzburg was better known for the movie, the Sound of Music, rather than Mozart! Nevertheless, we took a walk to Wolfgang's *Gebursthaus*, his house of birth that we visited. After some time for coffee and restrooms, on to the lunch stop at Melk, on the Blue Danube.

The company I worked for in those days contracted restaurants along the way. It was a great idea. We gave them a call from the morning stop, and they'd be ready for us when we got there, a couple of hours later!

But at Melk, the clients went in, they used the restrooms, and they walked out. A few looked at the menu, but Peppe and I were the only two having lunch! I can still see some of our clients sitting on the curb, right in front of the restaurant, waiting for us to come out again so we could leave.

Broke they were, very broke indeed…

In those days, in the morning, all they served was continental breakfast: a hard roll, sometimes very hard indeed, with a small portion of butter and a bit of jam, apricot or strawberry; usually, you also got some sort of oven-defrost deep-frozen croissant. This is what I called the daily plastic breakfast… In other words, they starved! The lack of a proper breakfast was bad enough, but to make things worse, they were getting very, very tight moneywise. And so, although they were really hungry, they skipped lunch!

We made it to our hotel in Vienna without getting lost, a miracle.

Actually, we almost made it to our hotel…

The rear half of the bus, from the middle door all the way to the back was one and a half feet higher than the front half. The elevated roof extension allowed the people who sat in the rear to sort of see what was going on up ahead. Unfortunately, that bit was too high to go under the railroad bridge! We could see the hotel, a hundred meters away, but we couldn't get to it! We had to drive around until we found another way!

The hotel had a great pool, and the entire group enjoyed the refreshing moment! A few of them headed for the bar to get a nice cold bier!

City tour, afternoon excursion, a waltzing experience at the Kursalon, a great local venue, and, in the evening, I ran an optional dinner in Grinzing, a famous wine village right outside Vienna, with plenty of joyful music!

The following day was one of the longest ones of the tour, but there were going to be several more of those! Vienna Venice, for a one night stop! There was no freeway in those days, just the regular road, and timing was of utmost importance!

We stayed in Mestre, right outside Venice. It was quick and easy to get to on arrival, especially from Vienna, and it was quite handy to get into the city in the evening, for the not-to-be-missed Gondola Serenade, although, arriving from Vienna, it was very, very late!

The next day promised to be somewhat of a rush. First thing, in the morning, we got on the public steamboat, the vaporetto, to Saint Mark's Square, with the locals, at rush hour: a bit crowded to say the least! On arrival, a short guided walking tour, then a visit to the glass blowing factory, the same one I'd gone to when I was in Venice with my mom, a few years before.

After some time for window-shopping and an early lunch "at leisure", grab-a-sandwich-and-run, we rendezvoused at the foot of the Campanile, the usual meeting place. It's tall enough that no one can miss it! When everyone was accounted for, we got on the vaporetto once again, and headed back for the bus; on to Zagreb, Yugoslavia, nowadays the capital of Croatia.

This is when the adventure really started, for good!

It was the summer of 1976. We had record high temperatures. The whole of Europe was suffering from a severe heat wave. There was no grass left in Hyde Park in London, none whatsoever, it was scorched; they still remember! It was bad up there, and it was worse down in the south! Everyone was hot and sticky! Thanks God, our Spanish bus, a Pegaso, had a great A/C…

We eventually got to the Yugoslavian border. Everything went fine, until the police asked my driver to see his passport. Peppe was Spanish, and the Spanish dictator, Franco had died a mere six months before. Due to the political tensions that still prevailed between Spain and the rest of the world, Peppe should have had a visa to get into Yugoslavia, a Socialist Republic at the time, but he didn't; he had no idea, no one had told him! So, there we were, in Trieste, driving around, looking for the Yugoslavian Consulate.

We found it alright, but it was closed. Consulates are always closed in the afternoon! There was a small café next door, and I asked to use their phone. I had to call my headquarters in Switzerland to report on the situation. Meanwhile our driver, Peppe was what-ever-he-was-doing, trying to find a solution…

I eventually got my office on the phone. It took well over an hour. In those days, there was no direct line, I'd had to go through an operator; no cell phones either of course…

Operations said I should call the Jolly Hotel in Trieste, the most expensive place in town at the time, and take the group there. This would have been charged to Peppe's company. They might even have contracted another bus and driver… which the clients would have strongly resented.

Well, we got lucky! While I was on the phone, Peppe found someone of the Consulate who stamped his passport with the magic open sesame! I called my people again to let them know that we were on our way to Zagreb, and I asked them to inform the hotel that we'd be late, and we were, very late indeed! It was well after ten, closer to eleven, when we finally arrived!

The manager was there, waiting for us, at the door of the hotel, with a welcoming smile on his face. While the porters took the suitcases up to the rooms, he served dinner on his own. Great dedication! A very nice man indeed. It turned out great. We were definitely very lucky...

And on the road again... Zagreb ended up a mere stop along the way, no time for sightseeing... On to Belgrade, nowadays the capital of Serbia, a short hop away. We took a little walk through town after an early dinner. The next day promised to be interminable, and it was.

Not only was the drive to Thessaloniki, Greece, a long one, another one of those, but when we got to the border, there was a time change: the Greeks were two hours ahead!

That's right, back in the day, not one country had the same time as the neighbor. No one had the same currency either! To make things worse, very few people carried a credit card. Plastic was not a currency yet! Modern travelling has changed all that! In those days, we stopped at every border to change money. Usually, we also changed time. Of course, some passengers always forgot to adjust their watch, so the next morning, they were either very early or very late!

We got to our hotel once again well after ten in the evening. This time, just to be sure, I hired a taxi to show us the way… Believe me, everyone was glad to get to their room after dinner, around midnight!

The next day, a Greek national guide met us at the hotel. The lady was going to be with us until Athens. I could breathe a bit! As for Peppe, he was looking forward to not getting lost anymore, at least for a few days, for as long as the guide was going to be with us!

In most people's mind, Greece is synonymous with a relaxing vacation, but we were on a tour, a very long and very tiring tour! In this case, vacation is what you do after the tour, when you return home!

The next overnight stop was Delphi, the center of the world for the ancient Greeks. It's a fabulous little town with loads of amazing sights, but, on the way, it was our guide's turn to get lost! Yes, she did! Peppe couldn't believe it!

We ended up in the middle of the square of a hilltop village, and definitely not on Mount Olympus with the ancient Greek Gods. It was the end of a narrow winding road. The square was quite small, and we had to move a few tables out of the way so Peppe could turn the bus around to get us back to the main road! He was not impressed! Everybody felt sorry for him. Nevertheless, everyone joked about it; the atmosphere was very joyous!

After the morning city tour of Delphi, mostly by foot, we headed for Athens…

…just fabulous, as always. Hot and sticky alright, but it felt soothing after the long and arduous past few days… and there were a few more of those up ahead! We were still very far from the end.

In fact, if you look at a map, Athens is the furthest city from London, where we started the tour, but also from Madrid where we were due to end…

Overnight Ionian Sea crossing, from Patras to Brindisi, Italy. It was spartan and most uncomfortable, but by then, they were so tired they could have slept anywhere! Actually, I used to call it "Ionian cruise", ironically, to make it sound better and more bearable!

After landing in Brindisi, we headed for Bari where we spent the night. The following day, on to Sorrento.

"Alan", (the same Brooklyn tone of voice!), "we need to change money!" This is all I heard the minute we left Bari! In the end, I told Peppe to get off the freeway and head for that small town, up there, in the hills! Let me tell you, he was scared! The idea of getting off the freeway and driving up in the hills reminded him of that small village near Delphi!

Well, we got there without a problem, but I can't remember that there was a bank! They didn't quite understand that in Europe, in those days, we didn't have banks all over, and worse even, that many banks didn't change money. The few that did had a special license. Then again, back in the day, there were no credit cards and no ATMs either, only cash and travelers' checks! In any case, the locals were very nice. They clearly didn't see tour buses pull in that often. Everyone took pictures, laughed, and stopped grumbling…

Lunch along the road, in one of those highway restaurants Italy was so famous for. They used whatever money they had. I'm sure they lent each other some of the precious Italian Lire! Yes, it could be somewhat of a pain if you didn't have the right currency! Before leaving Venice for Yugoslavia, I had insisted they get some Lire for when we returned to Italy, but some had obviously forgotten to do it; I knew some others had changed their Italian currency for Drachmas in Greece…

Nevertheless, it worked out. Somehow, it always does, doesn't it!?

Sorrento was welcoming! A touristy place for American tourists! Reassuring indeed! After dinner, some went to the Tarantella show at the Fauno Notte Club. For the younger ones, the place turned into a disco after the show…

Early rise, on to Capri and the Blue Grotto, weather permitting… Lunch in Anacapri, up there, at the top of the island, then, back to the boat and on to Naples, followed by a long drive to Rome… a heck of a day! Three nights in Rome.

Morning city tour, the Roman Forum and the Colosseum, the group picture at the Arch of Constantine, then the optional visit of the Sistine Chapel and the Vatican Museum, followed by a dinner excursion to Tivoli…

I loved Tivoli at night, with its illuminated gardens and hundreds of glittering fountains… A little slippery after a copious festive dinner, "a bit" of local wine, and a lot of dancing between the tables, but always a lot of fun for sure, and always a success! The next day was at leisure… There's so much to do and see in Rome!

Then it was an easy drive to Florence, across the Apennines, with a shopping stop on arrival, leather and gold, for those who still had a bit of money. Lunch break on Santa Croce Square, then we did the city-tour, by bus in those days. We finished on the other side of the Arno River, on the Piazzale Michelangelo, with a plunging view over Florence. They also have one of the two replicas of the statue of David up there, a favorite with the ladies!

Most of the economy tours stayed at the Hotel Mediterraneo, sort of downtown, close enough anyway. Dinner was a basic three course meal, including pasta of course, *penne al sugo*... After dinner, those who had enough energy took a walk to the nearby Ponte Vecchio...

This hotel was huge. It was used by several tour operators for their groups, and it was always busy. Guides and drivers ate together, in a quiet corner of the restaurant.

During the dinner, the Maitre D dropped by. He told us that a lady who worked for our company in New York was also staying at the hotel, and that she'd be happy to meet with some of us after dinner. The other guys had other plans so, I went ahead.

Her name was Ginny Powell. She was the manager of our New York office. We'll meet her again soon...

The next morning, at daybreak, as usual, up and away… We were ten, twelve days from the end of the tour. By then, all these very happy people were dead-tired-exhausted, wiped out, on top of being very, very, very broke!

The Leaning Tower… was still leaning! In those days, there were very few tourists. We parked right in front of it, across the street, just before the café-gelateria. It was the all-in-one stop, the wee-wee stop, the coffee break, the run-around-and-take-pictures stop, and most importantly, the last Italian ice-cream stop, etc… then, off again; on to the coast, past Carrara, where Michelangelo used to pick his blocks of marble…

To kill time, on the long and boring drive from Carrara to the Franco Italian border, I used to do a tunnel counting contest. Yes, totally silly! I believe there was something like 173 *gallerie*. Now, there is a major difference between a *galleria*, a regular tunnel, which counted, and a *galleria artificiale*, a covered roadway that only looks like a tunnel, and which therefore didn't count. It was just to make it more confusing of course, and hopefully more fun! We had three official counters. Since it was their duty to count, they were not allowed to sleep while everybody else was crashed.

Everyone wrote their name on a piece of paper, with a number between 150 and 200; then, at the other end, we made an average between the three counters' results, which were never the same of course! The winner got a bottle of Spumante! If they were two or more, they shared the bottle!

Getting to Nice, on the French Riviera, always felt like the ultimate experience, in the footsteps of the English gentry and the Russian aristocracy...

This time though, the A/C had broken down along the way. It had been a long, long, hot day, very long, and very hot indeed! Even the rocks and the pebbles on the beach in Nice looked appeasing!

Two nights stop, with the usual side trips: in the morning, Saint Paul de Vence and the perfume factory in nearby Grasse, and of course, in the evening, casino experience in Monte Carlo.

We used to stop the bus right in front of the main entrance, yes, just like James Bond! The doorman would stand there and open the door of the bus, "Good evening Sir"... and he'd help the ladies out. Oh, yes, these were the days!

Although the A/C was still out of order, Peppe was over the moon! The compressor his boss had sent to Nice by air from Madrid had not done the trick... but, to his relief, he was going to be back in Spain the next day. After six long weeks away from home, he could hardly wait!

It was the end of July, the beginning of August. The European tourists were driving down to the Costa Brava for their summer vacation. Let me tell you, it was busy. Getting across the border took a while, even more so without air-conditioning! At least we had windows and so, there was somewhat of a breeze when we moved! A brand new freeway had been inaugurated on the French side; it connected with the Spanish autopista, and it made things somewhat faster, just as well! We were moving slowly, but at a steady pace.

The driving day was so long we had to do four stops, morning stop on the highway on the French side, near Aix-en-Provence, lunch stop in town at Arles, then money exchange at the border, and one more comfort stop on the freeway on the Spanish side...

Eventually, Barcelona was on the horizon.

We stayed at the Hotel Terminal, across the street from the Sants train station. It doesn't exist anymore, the hotel that is! Nowadays, it's an office building. There used to be a garage on the ground floor, where Peppe parked the bus. The hotel reception was one up. I believe there was a prison on the other side of the street... not the classiest neighbor, but no one ever noticed! In any case, I went up to the front desk while the group waited on the bus. Actually, most of them got off, it was too hot and stuffy, and the day had been way too long, especially without A/C!

"Good afternoon, do you speak English", I asked the receptionist with my best smile. He looked like a descendant of Don Quixote, tall and skinny, with dark short hair and a thin moustache, like Franco, austere, tight-lipped, not even the shadow of a grin. In these days, the atmosphere was stern, it didn't allow for a joke, still the same as under the Spanish dictator… "Español", he replied curtly. "Français?", I ventured… I got myself the same abrupt answer! So, I used my best Castilian! In the end, after breaking the ice, which did take a while mind you, he turned out a nice man!

Without the A/C, the day had been very long and very hot. Understandably, the clients were getting a little cranky… They were happy to get to their rooms and jump in the shower! Some rushed to the bar and grabbed a cool beer! In these days, things were much cheaper in Spain, it helped!

Everything turned out just fine! Dinner at the hotel, city tour the next day, and Peppe helped me organize an afternoon Bull Fight excursion at the nearby bull ring, nowadays a shopping center! Optional Flamenco show in the evening, on the Ramblas, I believe everybody went!

The following day, short drive to Zaragoza, halfway between Barcelona and Madrid. There was no freeway at the time, and travelling on the regular roads in Spain could be a true experience!

The trucks couldn't go faster than 50, 60 km per hour, downhill that is; uphill, their speed went down to 15, 20km/h at the best! To make things even slower, most of the time, passing was not permitted… and of course, the police waited at the top of the hill! Nowadays, there's a freeway, so the groups rarely stay in Zaragoza. At the best, they stop for lunch and visit the Cathedral, quick, quick, as they operate an evening optional on arrival in Madrid!

In any case, after we arrived at our hotel, named after the local artist, the great Goya, I walked them to the Cathedral, Our Lady of the Pillar… Dinner at the hotel, Spanish time, late, and finally off to Madrid the next day!

One of the clients, by then a friend, was from Puerto Rico; he was a well known author, Robert Lewis. He travelled with his wife and two children, a girl and a boy, a lovely family indeed.

In the evening, Mr. Lewis and I would trade a smoke for a brandy. At the time, I loved those Cuban cigars, and they were so cheap in Spain. For his part, Mr. Lewis was well versed in the knowledge of the different varieties of the Spanish digestive liquor! His wife was not too happy about it, but there was so little time left!

Yes, it was "already" the end of the forty five days tour of Europe. Everyone was soon on their way home.

I spent a few more days in Madrid, at the same hotel, Hotel Praga. I had to wait for my next group to fly in, a few days later. Peppe was my driver once again. I believe he was not too thrilled to have to leave Spain!

For what I remember, the next trip was uneventful, nothing to write home about. I think I nearly lost someone in Capri, on 15 August, *Ferragosto* in Italian, the one day in the year when every single Italian goes somewhere. Due to the confusion in the port of Capri, one of my passengers nearly missed the boat!

A few days later, on another one of these super long days, Venice to Lucerne, we made an afternoon coffee stop at the top of the Saint Gotthard Pass, hot and sticky at the bottom, on the Venice side, and snow up at the top. The carrot cake was great! Nowadays, here too, there is a tunnel…

Bus tours have long lost their charm!

Then they gave me a special tour, a French speaking group of Acadians from Canada. They did a quick tour of France, from Paris all the way down to Carcassonne and back to Paris, a two week tour, once again uneventful!

Next, they had me do a 28 day tour, to finish the season! It might have looked as if they were testing my limits, but I couldn't care less! As long as I moved, I was happy, the rolling stone principle!

Moneywise, it was a catastrophe, but at least they provided both, food and lodging!

The 28 day trip, code named "M Tour", was very much like the 45 day, the "T Tour", except for Greece and Spain. To make it more interesting, I introduced a few add-on novelties of my own...

On the way to Hamburg, I organized a visit to a huge privately owned castle. One of my colleagues happened to be a genuine German Prince. He must have been either bored or ruined, or maybe both...

His aunt, I believe, was related to the Queen of the Netherlands. He had suggested that I make a stop there with my group. It was great fun. The Princess was most charming! She showed us around the castle herself. Everyone took plenty of pictures... Then we had lunch at the next door restaurant, very posh, a little expensive, but excellent food and great service, a real treat!

It was soon the end of the season. Winter was approaching, and it's definitely not my favorite part of the year. I have a problem with grey and cold. Nevertheless, at the time, I had a lovely girlfriend in London and I thought I'd spend some time with her, to polish my English... Well, it didn't work out!

I was back in Paris in no time, calling the manager of Capitol Airways to check if he had an empty seat on one of his flights to New York.

And I got lucky again!

A bunch of happy Parisians were heading for a three day pre-Christmas shopping spree in the Apple. I got one of the two empty seats on the plane. I sat next to the lady in charge.

The poor thing normally worked as a secretary. She had no idea of what she was supposed to do. Her boss had sent her on a free trip to New York in exchange for acting as the company rep, but she hadn't been briefed or anything…

So, I played travel-expert. I walked her through the details of the operation, like this guy had done, between JFK and Manhattan when I'd landed in New York for the first time, less than a year before! I told her about the announcements she should make on the PA system, what she should tell the people, the whole thing… There was plenty of time for that!

After we landed, I took a cab to the McAlpin Hotel where I'd stayed a few months before, but it was not a hotel anymore! The place was upside-down. They were turning the rooms into luxury rental apartments! Nevertheless, the security guy let me have one of the un-refurbished rooms for $10… in cash!

He woke me up the next morning at the crack of dawn, before the dayshift arrived! "You have to go now", he said. I grabbed a quick shower, and off to breakfast, next-door, on 33rd Street. I had to elaborate a plan! Ginny Powell, the manager of my company's New York office was at the top of the list!

I got on the subway to Forest Hills, Queens. When I came out, I hailed a taxi to go to Parker Towers. The cab driver drove... around the block! "Here we are!" he said, with a big smile on his face. Talk about being taken for a ride! That's when I learned the expression!

The doorman seemed a little surprised to see me with my suitcase that early in the morning, but he called Ginny. She was even more surprised to hear that I was downstairs in the hall! I went up the elevator; there she was, standing in the doorway of her apartment. She handed me a set of keys... "Come and meet me at the office at lunch time" she said, and she ran off.

That night, I had to meet the French lady from the plane. I didn't make it back to Ginny's place...

I popped in at the office the next day. During lunch, she said she was supposed to go to the concert that evening, but she wasn't feeling so well. As she hated the idea of throwing away the ticket, she suggested I go in her place. Sounded great!

That evening, I was at the Met. I'm not sure, but I think to remember they played some Tchaikovsky. Ginny and her best friend had season tickets, but neither of them made it. And so, I got to meet her best friend's daughter. Yes, I had been set up, a girls' plot! I didn't get back to Forest Hills after the concert... Oh, well...

Meanwhile, I had found a driveaway car, an old Dodge Dart which I had to take down to Florida. It was fun to drive and at least, it didn't use too much gas!

The lady owner was terribly surprised to see me so soon when I delivered her car, the day after I'd left New York. I'd barely slept! As a matter of fact, I think she was quite grumpy. I couldn't care less. I was in a rush to get to the beach! I left her place and got on a Greyhound to Miami, then another one to Key West, at the bottom of the Keys.

I decided to spend a few days at the Sea Crest, at the end of Simonton, until I found an apartment. I had stayed at Tom Dowd's motel earlier on that year, in March. It was the first place you would see as you came out of the beach. He had a huge blue and gold Visa Card sign hanging over the street in front of the motel. I couldn't miss that! At the time, I had been totally broke and my plastic card was the only currency I'd had left! I sure was glad my bank manager had insisted I take the card... (Don't leave home without it!)

On my first visit, in March, after renting a room for a few days, Tom had let me stay for free on a folding bed, in the storage room, next to the kitchen. In return, he asked me to make breakfast for a few residents! Best deal in town for sure! A couple more weeks in the sun, food and lodging free, in exchange for a bit of cooking…

One night, I actually cooked dinner for everybody! That was fun! Tom Dowd was a great guy, easy going, definitely the mood of Key West in those days, laid back and relaxed, no fuss! Great memories.

While I stayed there this time, I ran into this guy from Boston. Doug was his name. He rented this huge five bedroom house near the graveyard, on Olivia. He let me have one of the rooms for $100 a month. Couldn't beat that!

So, instead of spending the winter in cold grey London, with a charming girlfriend mind you, but still, I slept in the sun all day long, and I went out every single night, either playing pool or dancing at the local disco, the Monster!

My English improved tremendously, which was the idea after all. And thanks to the exercise I got, between the bicycle and the nightly dancing, I even got fit!

Ginny managed to get me a free ticket on Capitol to go back to Paris in March, and on I went for a second season of tour-guiding…

After one of those high school kids' groups, I was back on the regular tours... and what did I start with? Yes, the darn T Tour, the 45 days again, another one of those! I was definitely not impressed! It didn't leave many memories either... I wonder why!

The same tour escort from Hawaii was on it, with just a handful of clients this time; he had actually requested me! Thanks!

He also had some very odd customers. This one lady didn't like the way the toilets worked in Copenhagen and she blew a fuse! I mean, she really went up the wall! She and her husband flew back a few days later from Berlin, go figure! Strange people...

I have to admit, we did have some very peculiar customers in those days, a few crackpots for some of them. Some collected toilet paper from every place they went; they had a note book where they taped the paper on one page and wrote where it came from on the opposite page, with the time and the date! Others took pictures of the Coca Cola trucks we ran into. One took pictures of road accidents. Yes, some were definitely very, very odd to say the least!

After the T Tour, I got a three week tour, code named "P Tour", full load. That's when I realized that I could actually earn money while having fun. It was about time!

That's when my boss in Paris, Sigi, the Bavarian, got in touch with headquarters in Switzerland. His girl friend, Karen did the tour allocations, quite handy indeed! At his request, she gave me a string of so-called pajama tours: Europe in two weeks, 15 days, including the transatlantic flights, 14 nights in Europe proper, including one on the ferry between Holland and England.

The tour was especially designed for the American market where people usually have two weeks off a year. You add the weekend that precedes the two weeks, and you've got the fastest, most comprehensive tour of Central Europe... It was by far the most popular!

It got its nickname, pajama tour, from the fact that the clients had so little time to sleep at night. They had to catch up during the day, on the bus, while we drove to destination... no time to take their pajamas off so to speak!

As the pajama tour was far from easy to operate due to the extremely tight schedules, but also to the number of optional excursions that we ran on it, Sigi had me go parallel with a Swiss colleague from Lucerne, Pius, who briefed me at every step... Thanks to him, it worked out fantastic!

A few most important rules for this particular tour: after a brief "Good morning folks, this is where we go today and what we're going to do...", short and to the point, no more comments on the microphone whatsoever until the coffee break, none, they had to sleep! The best time to address the group was between the morning coffee break and lunch. Clearly, after lunch, they all napped, so, no blah, blah...

A little bit of strategy went a long way, and the result was visible: a happy outgoing bunch, or a half asleep yawning and grumbling one, for those of my colleagues who spoke too much and kept them awake unnecessarily!

Our clients flew off from the States on Friday night and landed in Europe on Saturday in the morning. Those who returned home took the same plane back.

We took the people who finished their tour to the airport and dropped them off in the departures area for check in. Then, we went to arrivals, picked up the new bunch and brought them to the hotel. The time it took to do the round trip, plus a brief information meeting and a welcome drink with the new ones, and their rooms were ready! Very well organized indeed, a well oiled clockwork!

The pajama tours went either from London to Paris, or Paris to London. The east coast customers flew into Paris while those from the west coast landed in London. One night stop everywhere, except for Paris and Rome, two nights.

That year, I worked nonstop, back-to-back, for seven months, from the high school kids in March, immediately followed by the 45 days T Tour, and the three weeks P Tour, not one day off until October. The pajama tours were all full, 52, 54 passengers, even 56 on one occasion! The 1977 season was dead exhausting: from 17 March until 17 October! After so many years, I still remember the dates!

One day, in Paris, Sigi asked me to take care of a special group. They spent a few days in Paris before going to London. The tour overlapped with both, the group I was finishing, and the group I was due to start. It was a bit of a mad house, to say the very least, but it worked out just great. The people were happy which is the main thing!

Then, in the middle of the summer, I was allocated another one of those high school groups, a very posh private Catholic school for girls. They travelled with three chaperones: two female teachers and a Sister. Every night, they took turn sitting in the corridor, for the entire night... The girls were wild I hear! During this tour, I remember Elvis died. And talking about pop music, their favorite album which they insisted I play on the sound system of the bus, was the "Bat out of Hell"! ... "I bet you say that to all the boys"... Yes, they knew the lyrics by heart!

The Sister was very watchful, she knew them well!

It was a very long and exhausting working summer! It felt good to head back for Key West at the end of the season!

In New York, I spent a few days with Ginny, but no more driveaway cars! I flew to Miami, with Pan Am, then with PBA, Princeton-Boston Airlines, down to Key West... Sea Crest Motel for a few nights, still $10 a night, probably a special price!

Then I found a small furnished apartment on South Street, around the corner from the Blue Marlin, between Simonton and Duval, a couple of blocks from the beach. The deal of the days, $110 a month, all inclusive, water and electricity! Yes, definitely the good old days!

That winter, Tom Dowd, the owner of the Sea Crest found himself without a breakfast cook. I think he had an accident or something. One morning he woke me up at the crack of dawn and asked me if I could replace him off the cuff, and so, I became the specialist of over easy, sunny side up, hash brown potatoes and the rest. It went on for a couple of weeks, until he found a real cook! The experience was fun!

The third season began very much like the previous one had ended, full speed ahead... After the usual high school kids group, I did the first pajama tour of the brochure, Paris to London.

Then I started getting bored. It's not a question of money, which was obviously very good, no, it's the lack of challenge! Repeat is not my thing, and money has never been my driving force! Doing the same "whatever-it-is", over and over again, quickly becomes utterly boring. It feels like going to the office, and this is definitely not my thing! I am more of a rolling stone. I have to catch the current and roll to the sea on the bumpy riverbed! Most importantly, I have to enjoy whatever it is that I do!

No fun, no can do!

During the next three years, from 1979 to 1981, I worked for a couple of friends: one in Germany, Axel, who operated a US West Coast tour company, Experiments in Traveling, with 18-25 age groups, great fun, and one in Paris, André, who ran the European operation of Trade Wind Tours, a Tour Operator out of Great Neck, New York. Both were à la carte rather than fixed menu. In addition, they gave me a lot of leeway to operate, as long as the clients were happy of course. Less money, but a lot more fun, and above all, no stress!

In 1980, with Trade Wind, I spent the entire season in and around Germany. It was the year of the Oberammergau Passion Play, a very popular event which always attracts loads of religious groups, mostly from the States. We spent two nights in Oberammergau, a small town in the middle of the Bavarian countryside, south of Munich, always with great pleasure.

While the driver and I were accommodated in a private house with some other colleagues, the group stayed with the locals, split over different families, two or four people per house, spread all over the village. A great experience for everyone!

Since the company had to fit the Passion Play within the itinerary, depending on the dates on which they had the reservations for, we were never very far from Oberammergau. The furthest was Venice, down in the south, Heidelberg and the Rhineland up north, and Vienna, Austria, on the east side… Lots of roasted pork-knuckles, beer, and pretzels that year, and plenty of Ludwig's Castles, mostly Linderhof near Munich!

I went to Key West in November, then André asked me to take a group of French bankers around the States for two weeks, from the Bonaventure Hotel in L.A. to the Caesar's Palace in Las Vegas, on to San Francisco, New Orleans and New York, farewell dinner at the Plaza.

I returned to Paris for Christmas, then I went to India for just over a month. I got back end of February, and I decided to move.

Paris had become too stressful and noisy. I rented a house in a laid back little town, thirty kilometers, twenty miles out of Le Mans, of the 24 hours car race fame.

That year, I went back to Experiments in Travelling. The kids were from "the Valley", north of L.A. or near there. They were easygoing, and we did nothing out of the ordinary. They had a great time, according to the brochure, plus a few especially concocted optional excursions here and there... all in all, an easy season.

Tour-guide work was minimal, but so were the expenses. For lack of revenue, I didn't go anywhere that winter, the first time in many years. After redecorating the house and planting some trees in the garden, I relaxed reading some sci-fi, the early stuff, the golden age as they say, Asimov, Simak, Sturgeon, van Vogt, and a few others. I even started writing a couple of books.... There are so many first chapters out there!

During the winter 1981-1982, both, Axel in Germany, and André in Paris went under, in the red, so, I had to get back to the mainstream guys...

Reintegrating the system can be somewhat of a challenge, but it worked out just fine, at the beginning.

I started the season with a couple of high school kids' tours for this other friend based in Paris, Leon. He ran this Falcon Tours/Cultural Heritage operation. On the second tour, while I was in Nice, I met this colleague who suggested I get in touch with his company in London, which I did. They gave me two 18-35 "Trendsetters". The second one was four weeks long, all the way down to Athens and back.

As much as I love Greece, the general feeling was far from ecstatic. Nothing to do with the clients who were great, but the management was totally unethical... The lady who made the tour allocations expected to receive presents in exchange for a tour! That place was a loonie bin. They went bankrupt one or two years later, just as well...

During the second Trendsetter tour, also in Nice, I ran into this friend of mine whom I knew from the early days, a Dutch guy by the name of Jaap. We'd known each other since 1973. He was a colleague and a friend of my former boss, Monsieur Peter. We finished on the same day in London, and he took me "by the hand" to his company's office. He served as my sponsor, my godfather, a requisite at the time! They asked me a couple of simple questions, "How do you go from Lucerne to Innsbruck?" sort of thing, and I went home.

A few days later, the telephone rang. My friend Jaap had been celebrating a bit too much in his hotel room near Venice. He'd walked out of his third-floor bedroom, mistaking the window for the door! Go figure… He was lucky he "only" broke "a few" bones. I believe he ended up with triple fractures on both legs. Nothing fatal, but he was going to be in the hospital, plastered from neck to toe for several months, six months I believe…

They asked me if I could take the tour he was supposed to do in September…

It was a great group, lots of fun, and darn good money, which was more than welcome. I was quite broke at the time, a recurrent habit of mine!

The tour started a bit awkwardly though.

In these days, we had to go all over London and collect the passengers from their hotel. It was a large group, 52. Not only did we have a lot of hotel pickups, but we had to return to the Departure Centre to take those who had arranged their own accommodation. Then, we had to do one more stop, on the way out, at the Tower Hotel. We spent so much time driving around that we left very late…

When we finally got to Dover, from the top of the hill, some distance away from the coast proper, we saw our Ferry as it was sailing out of the port to Calais…

"No panic" I told the group, "we'll take the next one." And so we did, but there were no cell phones in those days, and the driver on the other side of the Channel had no idea what was going on! So, we were a couple of hours late, and he was sort of moaning and groaning when we finally got there...

After I told him about our program in Paris, the excursions we were going to run, meaning more income for him as well, he seemed much happier! We had the 52 do all the excursions on the 18 days Globetrotter tour, and they were all extremely happy! So was George, our Belgian driver, nicknamed for the occasion the King of the Road!

There was also this fabulous lady on the tour. Maria was her name. A couple of weeks after the tour, I landed in LAX. She had booked me a room in a small motel in Redondo Beach, a great week!

Then I went to Key West for a while. It was the last time. The prices had gone up and the crowd had changed, not for the better either. Lots of people were selling condos, a sheer nuisance. You couldn't watch the sunset, the one and only ritual in Key West, without being harassed by some pushy sales people

In any case, I now had a big house to go back to, in the French countryside.

The rest the winter was quiet: more reading, plenty of gardening, and some roaming in the nearby forests, hunting for mushrooms! I love those wild forest mushrooms!

At the beginning of 1983, I rang up the office in London to let them know I was available. It was a good idea that I called, they had totally forgotten about me! I got my allocations a few days later...

On the second or third tour that year, I had another one of those great drivers, Jean Massage. He was also from Belgium. It always helps to have a good working team in the front!

For some reason, on the second night in Rome, I didn't run the usual optional excursion to Tivoli; the garden with the illuminated fountains might have been closed at night. Instead, Jean and I had dinner at the restaurant next to our hotel. Half of the group was there! Franco, the owner offered us a bottle of wine, then the kids from the group got us one or two more. Yes, definitely a bit too much! We walked back to the hotel singing "Strangers in the night"!

My next door neighbor called the reception to complain about the noise. Oops! She was also a tour guide, but she worked for the competition! Oh, well...

On that tour, I ran into this very nice girl, Christine was her name. She was very pretty and very intelligent, a great combination. Nothing happened, but we kept in touch.

In the spring of 1984, before the season started, I flew to L.A. to visit her, but also my friends in Carmel whom I hadn't seen since 1976... It was just before the Olympic Games. I was stopped for speeding near Santa Barbara. When the officer saw my driver's license, he said, "Oh, one of those!" He let me off with a big smile and a simple warning...

At the time, I enjoyed shopping in thrift stores. They had great clothes, fabulous quality and style, and so cheap. Nowadays, all the good stuff goes straight to the vintage shops where it sells for mega-bucks.

Well, in those days, I had the greatest clothes for next to nothing, and a brand new wardrobe for the season like no one else had! I shipped big boxes home, surface mail. They took six to eight weeks to get there. I used to work it out so they'd arrive after I got back! So, this time again, I shopped in every town between L.A. and Carmel. I'd take the yellow pages, mark every single store on a city map, and check them all out, one after the other, methodically!

I was quite serious about this lady in L.A., but I didn't want to start something I wouldn't be able to finish so, I promised her I'd be back, and off I was for another busy season.

Busy and chaotic. I got a bad ear infection. I ended up with a torn eardrum, painful to say the least. I asked the office for some time off, to get it fixed, but they wouldn't give me any. So I quit.

By then, the 18-35 were getting on my nerves: exhausting, demanding, and quite ungrateful... The lady who did the tour allocations was not too happy, far from it, but she finally gave me two weeks off. Unfortunately, it proved too short to get my ear fixed. It would have to wait until the end of the season. In any case, after the two week break, she gave me some real tours. No more Globe-Trotters!

At the end of the 1984 season, I realized it was cheaper to travel to some all-inclusive hotel on a beach somewhere rather than drive to the French coast for a week. So, I ended up spending five weeks in a small hotel in the Seychelles, right on the beach. My favorite pastime: I slept in the sun and swam all day, for a next-to-nothing bargain price. They had some huge promotions, it sure helps!

When I got back, I did a winter tour, two weeks, which finished in Paris at the very beginning of January. Then I went to the hospital to have my ear examined... but the surgeon decided to operate my nose instead! I'd had a motorbike accident back in 1970, a fairly bad one, and my nasal septum hadn't been repaired properly... My eardrum would have to wait one more year!

Because of my nose operation, I couldn't go to L.A. to see my friend. I promised I would go at the end of the 1985 season. It was decision time. Get married or bust!

… and bust it was. Once a rolling stone, always a rolling stone! One morning, I left a message on the table and drove off. I spent the rest of the time visiting succulent plants shops, in Palm Springs first, then on the coast, in Buena Vista. I met some great people along the way. I also mailed two or three big boxes of thrift store clothes to myself…

I got home two or three weeks later with a few fabulous succulent plants. I also found a few messages on my answering machine. I called her back. We had another long conversation, but she still insisted that we meet. Actually, she said she was going to come to Europe and travel for a couple of months during the summer…

Then I went to the hospital and I finally got my ear fixed. They did a skin graft on my ear drum. It's been more or less OK since then! Swimming, diving, and body surfing are great fun, but my ears have been complaining for a long time!

Shortly before the spring of 1986, two or three bombs blew up in Paris. What had promised to be another busy season went dead from one day to the next. Tabloids announced the beginning of WWIII and scared the travelers away. Christine decided to postpone her trip to Europe, while I was wondering when I would start working.

To make things worse, as if it were not enough, it was also the year Chernobyl blew up!

I finally got some work in September, and Christine flew in with her mom to meet me in London, at the end of my last tour. At the time, I always stayed at the Kensington Close, an economy hotel. I had reserved a room for them next door, at the Tara, much classier.

I invited them to my favorite Italian restaurant, not far from the Chelsea Bridge, one of the finest in London, a truly nice place. At the end of the dinner, I took them back to their hotel.

Christine and I had a long chat while playing Backgammon at the bar of the Tara. That's the last time we saw each other. No one shed a tear.

It had been somewhat of a bumpy year, money was scarce, but I needed a vacation. A few days after I got home, this lady friend called from Johannesburg, South Africa. She invited me to come and spend some time at her place. It was summer over there, so I caught some sun in her garden! I also picked up a few great plants from the nearby nursery.

Then, this former travel agent I had had on a tour the previous year asked me to come to Quebec City to teach a Tour Guide course. I got there at the beginning of December. It was fun, although a winter in Quebec can be quite a challenge for a sun worshipper!

The years were going by, tour after tour, dozens and dozens of people, some happy, some not so happy, some great fun, others not so much… I was settling into a routine, and that, I have a hard time with.

Towards the end of October, 1989, this lady approached me at the hotel where we stayed in Beaune, the Burgundy wine capital. She introduced herself as a headhunter. The man she was with was one of two brother-owners of the wine merchant company she was recruiting for. They were looking for a sales person for the export market. She offered to meet me in Paris a week later.

She filled my résumé for me, transforming a few things so they looked more glamorous. A few weeks later, I was driving to Burgundy to meet with the other brother. He was the boss.

He showed me around the wine cellar, huge and impressive, filled with thousands of naked bottles of both, red and white. He explained that the labels were placed on the bottles at the time of delivery so they didn't get damaged by humidity. Except that there were lots of different wine appellations in there, at vastly different prices, and it seemed to me that it would be awfully easy for the seller, and most unfortunate for the buyer, if high end wine labels were stuck on ordinary wine bottles… accidentally of course…

So anyway, it was an opportunity to try myself at something new, and I started working shortly after. When they told me I was going to go to Japan, I couldn't believe it! I had been collecting Japanese woodblock prints for some time, and I had transformed part of my garden into a Japanese garden! I am still a big Japanophile!

I flew to Tokyo with the guy I was supposed to replace. We stayed at the Akasaka Prince hotel, very posh indeed. My colleague explained it was a matter of representation. Meeting clients in a dump would be bad publicity! After lunch, on the day we arrived, he went to sleep and I took a walk outside, to sample the atmosphere. It usually takes quite a bit to surprise me, but I have to admit I was astounded!

A couple of days later, I noticed the Rolling Stones were going to perform in Tokyo. I thought it would be great if we could get tickets. My colleague told me that the owners of the stadium where the concert was taking place were clients of our wine company. He gave them a call, asking if and where we could get tickets. In a most honorable Japanese manner, they told him to come to their office at such and such a time on the day of the concert.

We ended up in the manager's box, way above everything, with an eagle's view of Mick Jagger & Co. They brought us some snacks and drinks, a couple of the finest bottles of wine, white and red, that they had acquired from us. We received a truly incredible welcome. I was extremely impressed... until I tasted the wine. What it said on the label, Clos Vougeot Grand Cru for the red, one of the finest and most expensive wines in the world was not, whatsoever, what was in the bottle, most definitely not. My colleague motioned me to keep quiet... I was horrified and shocked.

On another occasion, I met with the buyer of a major Japanese firm who had also bought some wines from us. He said the bottles showed some obvious flaws, adding that he had mentioned it to my colleague, but he'd never heard from him again... I started realizing that the wine business was perhaps a little crooked... at least the people I was working for.

It was not long until we separated.

After I managed to approach the one and only national importer and distributor of alcoholic beverages in Japan that didn't have a line of Burgundy wines, my boss told me I had become redundant and obsolete. He used more violent words, but the result was the same, "Hasta la vista baby!" He signed the contract with the Japanese, and a few days later, he sacked me! He saved on both, my salary and on the commissions he would have had to pay me!

It was not over yet...

I couldn't possibly know it at the time, but...

One evening, as I was watching the news, a number of years later, I was surprised to see the face of my former wine boss on national TV. He was telling the reporters who interviewed him that he had done some wrong things in the past... No, really? Did I indeed know it!

He had been indicted and convicted of fraud and a few other things in the same line... He actually pleaded guilty! He was forced to get out of the wine business and cede his company for next to nothing. Officially, he avoided jail time because he was too old; the rumor had it though that he knew people in high places who protected him... That's right, the French Revolution did not resolve all the problems!

So anyway, after I got out of the wine business, in June 1990, the rest of the year didn't get any better. The tourist season was going full speed ahead, but I was left on the roadside, standing in the dust as the tour buses drove by!

Since I'd told my boss I quit, he wouldn't hear about me! Fair enough...

I had bought my house in 1985. I had a mortgage to pay, but no revenue anymore. I had to find a solution.

So, I called the bank. The lady at the other end said, "Sure, no problem, we'll postpone your reimbursement for a year."

Shortly after, I sold the house and returned to Paris, more adequate for work.

It wasn't long until I was reinstated in my former job as a tour-guide. This time, they gave me regional tours, France and France and Spain, no European tours anymore. Just as well, they had become a total rat-race. We had to hurry all the time, and even if we got there first, we still had to get in line and wait everywhere, worse than the rush-hour in the subway… a nightmare.

The seasons were busy, sometimes working through the winter as well. As soon as I had a break, I'd fly someplace to sleep in the sun! Lying in the sun is a form of meditation; you close your eyes and stay still, and you review the past, one event at a time, some sort of recapitulation. In the end, getting a suntan is only a collateral activity!

At the end of the 1994 season, since it looked like I was going to do a lot of tours in Spain, I thought I'd improve my Spanish. During the summer, I had run into this flight attendant in Nice, on the French Riviera. She'd told me about a Spanish course she had done in Oaxaca, Mexico. I thought it would be a great opportunity to do both, get a taste of Mexico, and get my Spanish up to date!

I got my visa and took off at the end of December, right after Christmas which I spent with my mom.

The course was due to start at the beginning of January, so I had a bit of time for sightseeing.

Oaxaca is a great little town, lots to see, in and around, great food, and wonderful people. I spent five or six weeks there, then on to Puerto Vallarta for a few days. After that, I hopped along the coast and inland, by bus, heading for Tucson, Arizona, where I visited some friends.

I got back to Paris just in time for my first tour of France & Spain. The itinerary was excellent, the customers were most agreeable, and we had fabulous hotels... It was a very enjoyable season, away from the near chaos that prevailed in other parts of Europe, a lot less money, but who cares!

In 1995, British Airways was offering round the world tickets at a bargain price. It's not the plane that costs, but the hotels once you get there, unless you have some contacts, and I had a few!

New York was kind of cold, quite normal in December! I stayed at some friends', downtown, long enough to have a few toasted (charcoaled!) bagels and cream cheese, my favorite! Then I flew to L.A. I love L.A., I always have! I was there for a few days, so I rented a car and drove to Carmel to visit my long time friends. Yes, it was somewhat of a pilgrimage. It was the last time too!

The flight to Sydney, Australia, was way too long, extremely tiring, and I got myself in trouble with the authorities when I got there.

It was very late in the evening, and I was totally exhausted. I somehow didn't declare all the money that I had, accidentally, I clearly had nothing to hide. I believe they had a fairly low legal limit, and I was slightly over it, a few hundred dollars, less than a thousand for sure!

Even if they were "just doing their job", they were unnecessarily offensive, treating me like I was some kind of criminal. In the most hostile manner, they threatened to refuse me entry and confiscate my money. I was outraged, but I kept my temper.

After well over an hour, maybe two, they finally let me off... It was the rudest and most inhospitable reception I ever had in over fifty years of travelling all over the world, and most definitely not one to ever make me want to go back! Ever. Most aggravating indeed.

In any case, I spent over two months over there. It's a huge country! After a few days in Sydney, I started using my bus-pass. First stop Adelaide, then Melbourne. I had some friends there. I spent a week with them. Then, on the bus again, I headed for Ayers Rock, with all the tiny sightseeing stops along the way.

I made friend with the bus driver. He was with us for four or five days, and we used to have a beer or two in the evening after dinner, a very Australian tradition! I stayed at a great hotel at Ayers Rock, The Sails I believe it was called. They had a huge pool, just what I needed for a few days! Then, I thought I'd skip the bus and fly instead, at a discount price for foreign visitors.

I spent some time in Cairns, then in Brisbane, and on to Airlie Beach where I boarded a small old fashioned sailboat for a few days cruise, to see the Whitsundays and the Barrier Reef. Unfortunately, the weather was far from ideal and we couldn't dive. We couldn't even swim because of the deadly jellyfish. We slept on the deck and as it constantly threatened to rain, I started getting a bit agitated. I asked to shorten the cruise and return to shore.

After a week or so at some little motel with a pool, I headed south along the coast, down to Noosa, for a few more relaxing days, as always, at the pool, and then, finally, back to Sydney. It was a heck of a trip. I would have needed two or three more months and a fair amount of money to visit the western part… in another life, maybe!

Next destination, Osaka, Japan. A friend I had met in Oaxaca, Mexico, the year before was teaching English in a school there. As she was going to go back to the States for a couple of weeks to see her boyfriend, she let me have her apartment in Nishinomiya, halfway between Kobe and Osaka.

It was fun to be back in Japan, without the pressure of the wine business... I had all the time in the world to visit a few Japanese gardens, go to Kobe of course, and even to catch up with some local friends... I love Japan!

Everything has an end. It was time to return to Paris and then rush to London for the pre-season company meeting.

One after the other, the years were going by, the routine, French tours, France and Spain…

European tours were becoming so hectic that some colleagues started asking for regional tours. Some of them knew someone in the office, so they were allocated the tours that a few of us had made both, profitable and popular, and we ended up being pushed aside. I don't like that. Nobody does!

Incompetent management, inept Directors of Operations, one after the other, destabilized the team so their protégés got what they wanted, although they had no idea what they were doing, nor did they have any particular knowledge of the area; some didn't even speak the language! The atmosphere was getting lethal.

That's the time when the CEO, a former accountant, most frustrated in his early days in the company, back in the 70s, started hiring people like himself, envious, avid, and mean, devoid of any sort decency and good manners.

This one particular newcomer was known for fraudulent bankruptcy and other shady business practices she had managed to get away with in the past…

She was hired as a mercenary agent, and she came with her most devoted assistant. Her official task was to save money, at any cost it seems. She started contracting cheaper hotels throughout France and Spain, some of which quickly proved very unsafe.

Suddenly, we had people getting robbed, in Paris, in Madrid. In Seville, one of the hotels that we used smelled so bad that some clients threatened to sue the company. At least on one occasion, one couple refused to stay in what they called "a dump". They booked a room in another hotel! It was a nightmare.

Another place we stayed at in Paris lacked proper emergency exits in case of fire... I was able to get rid of it... but she held a grudge for years until she hit back. An evil witch...

She had recourse to systematic overbilling. The hotels and the restaurants that accepted such shady deals were places we would never have used otherwise. The method was at least dubious. It had an air of money laundering...

They were just a bunch of petty crooks, corrupt management all the way to the top, the perfect example of the worst of the financiers of the 1980's. At the time, it was a trend!

Money, the smell of money...

Yes, it was time to go, but we didn't have to do it.

The new Director of Operations sacked all the old ones, by waves, fifteen, twenty at a time. No apologies or long letters, we simply didn't get any assignments anymore, and those that we had were canceled. They had some secretary send us an e-mail. On top of everything else, they were a mere bunch of cowards!

Somewhere along the line, it seems that life makes the decisions we have failed to make! Even if it hurts, at the beginning, it usually is for the better!

A few twisted tour operators later…

One of them from the U.S. who ran both, land tours and river cruises told me that in Beaune, Burgundy, they didn't take the groups to the historical center when they did a mustard tour in the outskirts of the city because they sold the visit as an optional excursion on the river cruise, a few days later! What can I say?

I called the mustard company and changed the schedule for their included visits. I hear it caused some pretty serious havoc!

Another one, also a bus-tours and river-cruise operator, from Australia this time, published a glamorous European brochure valid for two years. They promised the newest, largest and most comfortable boats on the Rhine, the Main, and the Danube, but when they started their operation, the boats were not even built!

To make things worse, on the bus-tour part, prior to or post cruise, some travelling days were so badly planned that the driving hours exceeded the legal limit! In spite of the very generous salaries we were paid, two of us quit after a couple of tours!

Another one again, a land only operator from the States, newly arrived in Europe, concocted itineraries by borrowing ideas from the competition's brochures, the copy/paste principle! They used a piece from this one here, and a piece from that one there... just like Frankenstein's monster! They not only didn't know Europe, but they had no idea how to operate a tour. They clearly didn't seem to care either. Of course, it was a catastrophe... Again, I quit after two tours...

The list is long of those crooks who abused their customers, publishing a lovely colorful brochure, full of great pictures and lies, relying on professional tour guides to save the situation, once on the road at destination...

Mind you, it was nothing new either. In 1985 already, I was allocated a special tour with a group of French Canadians from Quebec. Ironically, the tour was called "The Connoisseur". The itinerary was totally extravagant. Some parts were just plain inventions; several included features simply did not exist! I couldn't believe what I read when I laid my eyes on the printed itinerary...

It was so bad that, at the start of the tour, I had to tell the group to forget about the brochure! I assured them I would do whatever I could, to the best of my ability, but for the rest, they'd have to talk to their travel agent when they got back...

This Canadian tour operator that the company I worked for at the time handled in Europe went under during the following winter... The rumor had it that the CEO took off with the money... another fraudulent bankruptcy... to avoid lawsuits I suppose!

Tourism has always been a lucrative business, but with time, it became a grey industry. Many of those who were running it until recently had no moral standards. They were greedy and ruthless. Service was the least of their concerns. Profit was all that mattered.

The smell of money, like the smell of blood...

Nineteen eighty two was the beginning of Act Two of my tour guiding life. Me, the wild rolling stone, with a passion for what I do, with an absolute fixation on quality and a job well done, impossible to harness and never accepting a compromise, and they, obsessed with fast bucks and a cheap profit, and clearly not willing to put up with any of my moods, no matter how justified!

Back in the day, most of us were sort of wild characters out of a black and white comic book, with strong exaggerated features... Over the years, the management changed, the clients changed, and yes, the times changed. Only problem, we didn't!

So, from then on, it was a long series of me quitting, they asking me back, they sacking me and having me back again, and so on and so forth, for thirty years... I hear some married couples do that too!

Well, we eventually got divorced... until next time I suppose, although now, with the Coronavirus, we can say, almost for sure, that there isn't going to be any next time.

Yep, as it says, "That's all folks!"

As a consequence of the pandemic, this travel saga will never resume, at least the way it was operated until a few months ago, just before the winter of 2019-2020.

I had come in on the European tours in 1976, on the occasion of a company shakeup. Long story…

They had apparently bought a small cruise ship, yes, already then! Several tour groups were booked on the cruise, as an extension of their land tour. I understand it was sold out and ready to sail but, as the buses were driving into the port of Genoa, Italy, the ship sunk… so I was told.

The following year, as they had to recoup from the financial misadventure, a total fiasco, they tightened the Tour Managers and shrunk their income. Some got pretty mad in the process! They tried to set up resistance. A few even planned a strike! But again, in those days they had no cell phones, not even faxes! Ultimately, they were defeated for lack of proper means of communication…

To make up for those they sacked, following the failed mutiny, they hired a bunch of new people. I was one of them. In total, there were three training tours the year I joined, three times eighty-ish applicants! They didn't look for great knowledge or imposing personalities, no, just easy going gals and guys, able to keep the customers happy, to sell them the company optional excursions, and promote the shops where they got a commission, in addition to a few other sources of income, mostly in cash in those days. The idea was to make up for the Genoese Titanic!

In the process, they also changed our title, from Tour Manager to Tour Director. We didn't manage anymore; from then on, we stood as the public image of the company. We had become the reps!

The Tour Managers had an association which I joined in 1977. In those days, being a member was a proof of integrity and professionalism. Just in case, we had a little leaflet titled Ethics & Principles. Back in the day, some tour operators belonged to the association as Associate Members, meaning that they agreed to abide by the same principles. That's a long, long time ago! After a while, they didn't renew their membership anymore…

As long as the tracking technology that we know now had not been introduced, let alone invented, the laptops, the smart-phones and all of that, we could still maneuver around… and manage! And so we did, responsibly.

On top of the regular company optional tours, we also ran so-called "black" excursions, to places that we knew well, they were our own. We gave our customers tremendous value for money, adding depth to an otherwise long and tedious drive, a mere sleep-on-the-bus tour, hence the well known phrase, "The tour manager makes or breaks the tour." At the same time, we improved our revenues and those of the bus drivers, merely making up for what they had taken away from us!

When I joined this last company, in 1982, we were just a handful, 30, 35 of us, a small family of "old boys", and a few girls too. Most of us had known each other for a number of years! We ran our tours our own way. We picked our local guides and our optional venues, even the exchange rates! There was no such thing as company infringement, but things changed.

They started hiring "new ones", to destabilize the "old ones", mind games. As some of these new people were quite wild and unfortunately lacked both, ethics and principles, regulations had to be introduced... and here too, we became Tour Directors! Then, in 1985, the boss, the former accountant introduced a levy: we had to pay to work! That money went to the Bahamas where I believe he had some property...

When they shot "The Night of the Iguana", the movie, back in the early 1960's, the groups were small, 28, 30 at the most. The luggage traveled on the roof and there was no A/C: the buses had windows! Nevertheless, they were luxury tours: the clients had style.

As the cost of transatlantic flights was out of reach for ordinary folks, very few people travelled to Europe, and so, there were very few groups. The scarcity of the tours, but also their quality made them desirable and valuable. The only publicity needed was the word of mouth, and they were all full.

Then, three novelties were introduced, charter flights, vacations bank-loans, and credit/debit cards. There was actually a fourth one, a major one in fact: TV ads. If you were around in the 70's and the 80's, you might remember some of those prime time game shows. The prize they offered to the winner was a first class tour of Europe for two.

These innovations, led to astounding changes, and not just in tourism. They simply transformed the world, the whole world, seriously!

The first novelty was the charter flights. They revolutionized non-corporate, leisure travel. The unreachable dream suddenly became affordable. As with the automobile industry, and thanks to the Ford model T, back in the day, tourism suddenly also became an industry. Consumerism led to mass travel!

Then it snowballed.

First, it gave a huge boost to the airplane industry, Mac Douglas, Boeing, Airbus and a few others. Then the infrastructure: hotels and restaurants were built all over, with whatever money, the source being often grey at the very least.

The best example of this exponential expansion is probably Las Vegas that went from bad boys' town to a respectable family resort! How amusing indeed! Well, the same applies to so many places all over the world.

Like in Las Vegas, everything that connected directly or indirectly to the tourist industry kept expanding, with a few hiccups along the way, one with each crisis that came up…

As for the tour operators, travel groups and the rest, the well managed pioneer family-run businesses grew to become multinational concerns. A few were lost along the way, as well as some airlines… mostly those that couldn't adapt to the low-cost concept.

To make the dream-vacation come true, the banks played along. Many of the customers on my first tours had borrowed a fair amount of money to purchase their once-in-a-life-time trip to Europe, the land of their forefathers...

Last, and definitely not least, the credit/debit card helped them cope with the extra-expenses, once they got there... the shopping, the non-included meals, and the optional excursions.

Before the introduction of the plastic card, (don't leave home without it!), they had to call some friends or family members back home and ask them to transfer money to a town where we would be seven to ten days later; that's the time it took in those days! It also had to be a place where we had a two night stop so they'd have the time to go to the bank and get the money. Last and not least, it mustn't be on a weekend of course, so the bank wouldn't be closed!

Yes, it was awfully complicated! In fact, on a short tour, it was simply impossible! So yes, plastic solved an enormous amount of problems!

In the 70's, when they started using charter airlines to fly their less affluent customers, the main Tour Operators started publishing two or three brochures, super-budget, economy, and first-class; alternatively, they were called economy, first-class, and deluxe... It was mostly the hotels that were different, from two stars to four or even five stars.

With time, the brochures got thicker, with a wider choice of itineraries, to appeal to different customers. Then, they started offering trips to the rest of the world. They acquired local companies which they used to run their overseas operations.

They became global operators.

Their clients came from all the continents, and, in the early days, transferring money from A to B was both, easy and discrete, using banks in grey countries...

This contributed to the development of group travel and mass tourism all over the world, but also to the establishment and the expansion of many local businesses, hotels, restaurants, name it... The snowball effect for the better cause!

Without this grey money, many well known landmarks would have shut down long ago, some wouldn't even exist for that matter! You have no idea!

Mind you, with the coronavirus crisis, many might not make it. In fact, we can already say that many will not make it. Some are already gone...

The image is the farmer shaking the plum tree to make the bad fruits fall... In short, let's call it the plum tree principle!

In any case, until sometime between the mid-70's and the mid-80's, in every sector of activity and not just tourism, pioneer entrepreneurs ran the businesses they had created. As they got older and pulled out, their companies were taken over by financiers.

These guys aren't known for liking poetry. They add two and two, and they subtract what's not profitable, in their eyes... Since they usually have no idea of the business they're dealing with, they cut the expenses where they shouldn't. As a result, the company loses its original spirit and it goes bust.

Like in every other business field, Tour operators' purpose is to provide a service. The pioneers, the founders of the various firms had a passion for what they did. Making a profit was the reward for a job well done... but the financiers are in a rush, they want the money first!

Fast bucks!

Unfortunately, a number of those rapacious sharks ended up in tourism, hired by gullible managers who were eager to make a few extra bucks... phony contracts, retro-commissions, etc... as long as they got their cut. It would be too tedious to enumerate all their deceptive embezzling strategies, but embezzling it was...

They stayed far too long, and they did an enormous amount of damage... and not just in tourism.

Meanwhile, everything had changed, once again.

The reshaping of the world economy saw the emergence of new nationalities on the travel scene, people we had never seen before, at least in such numbers, like the Chinese and the Indians, with a combined population of nearly three billion, and growing!

There were days, in Lucerne, Switzerland, you could have thought you were not in the Swiss Alps anymore but in the Himalayas, in Ladakh or in Kashmir!

Not only did the customers change, but so did the regulations.

The 45 day tour that I did twice back in the 70's would now be illegal, and those pajama tours even more so! The traveling days were too long, from the crack of dawn until late at night, sometimes late into the night, and there were too many consecutive driving days: the T Tour was 45 days long without a single day of rest for the driver! Simple enough, these tours don't exist anymore.

Due to these restrictive but necessary safety regulations, the itineraries had to be modified: shorter traveling days, more two night stops, replacement drivers at least once a week, etc… Naturally, the costs increased. Meanwhile, the average income of the average tourist had decreased and so, a number of potential customers were lost: there were fewer and fewer new customers.

Higher costs led to fewer travelers, which in turn led to even higher prices. This essentially concerned the bus-tours.

Not only did the price hike discourage new customers, but many repeat customers were also lost in the process. Those who used to travel to Europe every year or every other year didn't have the financial means any longer, but there's something else...

The main reason for the decline of bus-tours in Europe is much simpler: the repeat customers had become too old to travel at such a frantic rhythm. As a matter of fact, since the 70's and the 80's, many had actually passed away!

Among those who were still around, the few who could still afford a vacation just wanted to sit back and relax, to sleep in their bed at night, and not on the bus!

The concept of the bus-tour of the 70's and the 80's is simply passé...

These are a few of the reasons why people shifted to cruises which, in the meantime, had become much cheaper!

The other major change in global travelling habits is of course the internet. A lot of people decided to organize their own trips.

The internet somehow convinced them that they were travel experts! For most, they had no idea, not the slightest, but they were convinced that the World Wide Web would tell them everything they needed to know…

A friend of mine has a fixation with bridges. A few years back, she visited Cordoba, Spain. Strangely enough, she didn't know that there is a huge Roman bridge that crosses the Guadalquivir River, right in the center of town, next to the Mezquita. She missed it! When I asked her how she'd liked it, she freaked out! Go figure!

In the old days, as we drove around Europe for whichever length of time, between the included itinerary and the optional excursions, we showed our customers nearly all the sights. We worked very hard to make their "once-in-a-life-time" journey exceptional and memorable, for them of course, but also for the word of mouth, to build a clientele!

On the pajama tour, we had very little time to sleep but on the bus. We would arrive at the hotel in the outskirts of Venice around half past six, seven in the evening. We went straight to the dining room and had dinner while the porters took the suitcases upstairs. Then, after the clients had brought their hand luggage up to their room and brushed their teeth, we went out again, to Venice proper, to do the Gondola Serenade. We never got back to the hotel before at least ten thirty, eleven... and out again the next morning, at seven fifteen, seven thirty prompt! Mind you, the continental breakfast didn't take too much time!

We did the same thing nearly every day, and every single client did every single excursion... or else, what's the point?!...

As a consequence, they had huge extra expenses, hence the credit/debit cards. They gladly used them to purchase everything that was available, so they wouldn't miss a thing. They did it all in one go... "We're never going to be back..." is what they used to say. They were the first generation of bus-tour travelers, the same people as the characters of the movie, "If it's Tuesday, this must be Belgium"!

The next generation of tourists, those of the mid-80's onward were slightly younger. They also had more money, the middleclass and upper middleclass. They took a trip to Europe every year, every two years, to a different area. And so, from purely European, the whole of Europe, the tours became regional. After enjoying their first "escorted tour of Europe", as an introduction, they came back on a tour of Spain and Portugal, a tour of the U.K., of Italy, France, Scandinavia...

But then, as this new generation was getting older, we had all these disasters, one after the other. In

1986, we had two or three bombs in Paris. In some countries, eager to print sensational headlines to sell more printed paper, the press announced it was the beginning of WWIII… As a result, tourism crumbled.

Two of the main Tour Operators, both established exclusively on the American market crashed. As a rare few clients wouldn't cancel their trip, they had to run a few tours, but with barely anyone on board. Once, I saw a double-decker bus with only two passengers. They sat upstairs, above the driver and the tour guide; the rest of the bus was empty! No surprise they ceased operating at the end of the year.

One thousand tour guides, some employed fulltime some only part-time lost their job in the process, yes, one thousand! Not to mention the booking offices and the travel agents in the States, the restaurants, the bus companies, the hotels… all the businesses, hundreds of them throughout Europe that they'd had contracts with.

By the time things got better, around 1990, we had the dot-com bubble burst. So many people lost so much money. We lost half of our customers, the better part; those who still came after that were broke… but we got by. Then we had 9/11, then the sub-primes… what next? Ah, yes, the darn Coronavirus…

Even before the coronavirus crisis, the market had vanished! The few would-be travelers that were left had no money. They came to Europe on a low-cost flight and then, they were on such a tight budget that they couldn't afford a guided tour of Versailles or a visit to some well known vineyard followed by a gourmet dinner at a local restaurant. "It should be included", they kept saying, with a certain amount of anger in their voice, seeming to blame us, as if it were our fault!

They refused to realize that it would make the cost of the tour higher... and if it were, they would have booked a cheaper one with some low-cost self proclaimed tour operator, hence the long list of crooks!

They always proliferate in times of crisis!

Long before the virus, the customers had been lost, for good... They kept looking for cheap anything, and so, for most, they had moved to the cheap cruises! The more people on a ship, the cheaper the cruise!

Now, this is really scary! It's the best way to turn a lovely ship, (remember the Love Boat?) into an incubator!

The low-cost cruises!

Now this is a totally different product! On a bus tour, you visit, a lot. In fact, that's all you do. That's the purpose of the tour: you drive to all the sites, every single one of them that is worth seeing or visiting. You don't miss a thing!

On the other hand, on a low-cost cruise, you mostly sit there and stuff yourself in one of the all-inclusive restaurants, anytime you want. I believe at least one of them remains open 24/7. Then, you indulge in a drink or two at one of the bars before going to a disco or to a show. Or else, you may want to try your luck with the gambling machines… Las Vegas on the seas!

You may think I exaggerate, but believe me, not that much!

A cruise is definitely not the kind of travelling you want to do if you want to see the world. As the song says, "you'll see the sea"! Go to Vegas, take a gondola serenade under the Eiffel Tower or the Arch of Triumph, or alongside the Great Pyramid of Giza, this might be preferable! It's definitely cheaper, and you can check out and leave anytime you want…

The world has become somewhat lazy. No daily un-packing/re-packing, no early morning-call. Just a slow-motion journey on the blue seas…

…sitting at the bar, on the upper deck, sipping on an exotic cocktail, a straw hat on your head and dark sunglasses on your nose, gazing endlessly at the horizon, hoping it never changes. It's like sitting on a little cloud, up there in the blue heavens…

It has become quite cheap as well.

With ten thousand people on the same cruise ship, between the passengers and the crew, you sure cut down on expenses!

And I hear they were planning to build bigger ships!

They were…

Although all of this might sound either odd or gloomy, I believe there is still a future for land tours, for those who want to see things for themselves and understand the world in which we live. Clearly though, it can't be done as it was back in the 70's and the 80's anymore…

The super-tightly packed vacation contest is over, at least for legal reasons! First, the product, always more and faster, more countries, more cities, more sights, in the shortest possible time, run, run, run… And then, the container, always bigger, ten meter bus, 40 passengers, twelve meter bus, 52 passengers, fourteen meter bus, 60 passengers, double-decker bus, 72+ passengers, double-decker 14 meters, 80+ passengers… with an extra van in the back for the luggage! Crazy isn't it?

Mind you, it's the same for the airplanes! The Airbus A380 can carry up to 853 passengers! And yes, it's also the same for these super jumbo cruise liners!

Back in the mid-70's, on any given day, between Easter and October, there would be at the most 2 or 3 tour groups leaving Lucerne, Switzerland, for Innsbruck, Austria, around seven thirty, eight in the morning.

They headed for Vaduz, Liechtenstein where they stopped for coffee, downtown, next to the souvenir shop. There was only one parking, for three of four busses, and only one souvenir shop, bottom line.

Everybody got their postcards and their souvenirs from the shop, and then they went for restrooms and coffee in that big café-restaurant, across the street.

More recently, it was closer to 50, 60 buses, full load, every single day; so many people in fact that Vaduz was unable to accommodate them, not enough space to park so many buses, and definitely not enough facilities, coffee shops, restrooms, etc... So they made their morning stop on the freeway instead, at the restaurant next to the gas station. And they lined up of course! They were never less than four or five groups at a time, and none of them ever caught a glimpse of the castle.

So, we're back to where we started, before the introduction of the charter flights, and clearly, before the start of the coronavirus pandemic.

If there is a future for land tours, it is for smaller groups, which means higher costs; in turn, due to the price hike, there will be less potential customers and therefore fewer tours.

Smaller and fewer is the new trend.

In terms of itinerary, the groups should stay clear of the beaten track, away from the four lanes freeways, contrary to what the rushed tours were doing until recently. The rat race that they had become, more, more, more, faster and faster and faster must give way to a new concept.

In this matter like in many others, old is new…

There is little doubt that some tourists will still want to travel by bus, at least because it remains the best way to visit an area, but they will have to do it like in the old days.

They will have to use smaller vehicles, with the additional comfort of modern amenities of course, like the Wi-Fi and the A/C. On the other hand, onboard restrooms aren't necessary. On smaller roads, one is able to stop more often, at least to visit the sights! Size-wise, ten meter buses are perfect, not for forty people though, but eighteen to twenty five at the most.

Itineraries need to be changed. Out of the beaten track, smaller roads, smaller hotels, and no optionals: in the small towns, there aren't any! All-inclusive, meals and sights… This is the future of bus travel.

Instead of staying on the freeways and rushing to the next city to do an optional excursion on arrival, instead of having coffee breaks and lunches in highway restaurants where you have to line up behind three or four other groups, instead of flash-visiting the whole of Europe in ten or twelve days, the idea is to travel on secondary roads and discover, either an area, regional tours, or a theme, in the footsteps of… Hannibal, Julius Caesar, Napoleon I, but also Leonardo da Vinci, Van Gogh,

Monet or Picasso... or else, following one of the several routes of the Camino de Santiago.

There are so many fascinating options for those who wish to discover the culture and the history of a place... which is what tours are all about after all!

This way of traveling will be reserved for an elite, not a financial elite, although the tours won't be cheap, but a culture hungry elite, people who want to see, discover, visit, and not just brag with their neighbors or coworkers, the "been there, done that" kind of people, like so many of those who traveled in the last few years, who never knew where they were, but for the videos they had shot and the selfies they'd flooded the social media with...

This will require specialized tour guides, with in-depth knowledge and knowhow. There are many excellent ones, mostly those who have already done regional tours. They're from the area. They have great culture and historical knowledge, and naturally, they speak the language. They also know the local lore.

The prices need to be increased, but not much. Actually, some of the costs can be reduced: instead of using deluxe hotels, small privately owned countryside two or three stars will do. In addition, dining in the restaurant of the hotel and sampling the simple local cuisine would be an attractive feature while not being so costly.

On the other hand, the salaries of the bus drivers and the tour guides must be raised, to attract the best and keep them.

The price hike will operate a natural selection. Those who look for a cheap vacation will be lost. Mind you, they've been lost for quite some time already!

Some years ago, I had this most bizarre couple on a winter tour of France. They had booked a two-week vacation not knowing where they were going to go! First choice, Italy, second choice, Spain and Portugal, and third choice France, whichever would be available at the time of departure…

They had no idea where they were going to go or what they were going to do once they got there. They just sat on the bus, wherever it went! They didn't go for the sights, the history, or the culture, no, they just went for the price! Apparently, the empty seats were discounted shortly before departure, the last-minute vacation principle, sale and clearance! The worst of consumerism…

Travel agents have a basic set of questions for their clients: first, time and budget, "How long do you want to go away for, and how much are you willing to spend?" Then, the reason for traveling: sightseeing or lounging by the pool? The destination comes last. It depends on availability, but also on the criteria that they gave to their travel agent…

No wonder why so many people make their own arrangements on the internet!

One thing for sure, there won't be any such thing as cheap or discounted tours anymore. The regular tours weren't that cheap either.

Doing it by yourself could be quite expensive as well. I recently priced a tour of France for a couple of friends. Between the transportation, the hotels, the meals and the sights, a regular two week tour with any of the main tour operators would have been way cheaper and so much better!

They didn't make it either, too expensive!

On top of the recently introduced measures regarding the driving hours and more generally, the working conditions of the bus drivers, the new health regulations will eventually kill these crazy run-around trips.

As a matter of fact, they could kill the whole business altogether, at least the less recommendable tour companies, those who thrive mostly on misrepresentation...

Remember? ...the plum tree principle!

As a consequence of mass travel, of packing more people in airplanes, tour buses, and cruise ships, the various means of transportation have become mere incubators... The fact of the matter is, they already were before the virus, but the threat level has changed, lethally so...

A tour bus can quickly become a hospital on wheels, with a visiting Doctor every night, one hotel after the other. One sick passenger could contaminate a whole group in a matter of two or three days! On some tours, nearly every day, we'd have to call the reception ahead and ask them to book an English speaking Doctor for our estimated time of arrival ...

Then, while the group would be having dinner, we'd run to the pharmacy with the prescriptions. Later on that night, we'd be filling the insurance forms...

It quickly turned into a nightmare! Oftentimes, the clients who were sick had to stay behind, until they were able to go home again... The extra expenses were ultimately taken care of by their travel insurance, if they had one... Those who didn't usually insisted on rejoining the tour...

How it happened? Very simple... Usually, a passenger caught a bug on the incoming flight, on a plane where the air system was contaminated for lack of proper maintenance... No matter how strongly the airlines may deny it, this happened a lot more than you'd think!

Then, the sick passenger simply brought the bug on the bus. If the A/C filters weren't cleaned and disinfected or even changed every day, and the bus thoroughly sprayed every night, everyone got sick in a few days. At the end of the tour, they returned home coughing and sneezing their head off. This is a well known fact for all of us in the industry!

As a matter of fact, the same happened on several cruises at the beginning of the pandemic. Entire ships were quarantined, prevented from docking, and so many of their passengers fell ill...

Unfortunately, this darn virus is a lot more lethal than a head cold or a chest cold, and the consequences of a contamination would be much worse.

Because it has become terribly unsafe, but not only, the way tour groups used to travel belongs to the past. Mass travel, low-cost travel, on buses but also on airplanes, trains, etc... is not viable any longer. Mass tourism has indeed become obsolete. The question is, what next?

Well, if the economy recovers, when it does that is, and if people are still willing to travel, choices will have to be made. The various means of transportation, planes, buses, and trains will have to be totally safe, health wise... Naturally, the expenses incurred will have to be passed on to the customers. This will add up very quickly, on top of the costs of hotels, restaurants and sights. So, clearly, faraway leisure travel will once again be somewhat of a costly venture.

We can expect less airplanes up in the sky, which means that some airlines will default and disappear, first those which were already fragile, then those that relied exclusively on large numbers, like the low-cost companies...

Of course, the incoming/outgoing tour operators haven't integrated these changes yet. For most, they're still hoping to run their operation as they used to, not this year, in 2020, the season has been canceled, but from 2021 onward, with more or less the same numbers, and in roughly the same conditions as "before".

Not only are they ignoring the health risks their passengers could incur, but they're clearly not taking into consideration both the blow the economy will have suffered in the meantime, and the subsequent massive drop in potential customers…

Even if the exercise is not pleasant, because of its implications, I believe it would be reasonable to do some projections, to try and see where this crisis could lead.

Clearly, the year 2020 will not see a lot of long distance travel, if any at all… As a consequence, some operators and many service providers will disappear.

In addition, areas like the Pacific coast of Mexico, regions like the Yucatan, both the Riviera Maya and the archeological sites inland, countries like Greece and, to a lesser extent, France, Italy, Spain, and Portugal, and so many more indeed all over the world, which rely on tourism to support their economy will suffer a major blow.

This, in turn, will impact a large number of people, locally first, and eventually worldwide, because like tourism, everything is connected and global.

Because of uncertain health conditions, at home and at destination, hundreds of thousands of Chinese and Indians, and millions of westerners, from North

America, Australia, New Zealand and Europe will not travel.

Clearly, those without a job or whose situation is critical will not travel either…

In turn, all the people who depend on them for their income, the shop keepers and the service providers, both at home and at the destinations they would have gone to otherwise won't be working either.

They will constitute the second wave of unemployed which will appear in the fall of 2020… and it goes on…

We can expect a snowball effect, and no one knows where and when an avalanche will stop… Usually, it is at the very bottom of the mountain.

No matter what, the damage will be massive, and things will never be the same. Anyone trying to go against the current will disappear. Some already have.

In 2019, before the pandemic, several low-cost airlines and tour operators, including some well known names went bust, and for a very simple reason indeed: you can't sell something for less than it costs! You have to make a profit, at least to cover the expenses!

Going against all common sense, which is really unbelievable on their part, some travel companies relied entirely on the customers who paid their vacations in full ahead of time to have enough cash to run their daily operations! How mad indeed! Well, they're gone... Unfortunately hundreds of people lost their job in the process...

Well established airlines are taking drastic measures in order to survive. Several are in the process of letting go of thousands of workers. This will have consequences of course. Behind each person laid off is a family...

One of the first consequences is the aerospace companies cutting their workforce and getting rid of thousands of employees worldwide...

The near future will tell if people are willing to travel, locally or far and wide, in which conditions, and at which price.

In any case, during the coming fall of 2020 and the following winter, we will see a number of companies go under, in tourism and transport, but also in the related service industries, restaurants, hotels, etc... which will then impact other businesses, by ricochet... connected and global.

By the spring of 2021, or at the latest at the beginning of the summer, we should be able to assess the extent of the damage.

By then we should know what to expect, a turnaround and an improvement of the situation, no matter how small, or a second wave of economic downfall of unknown magnitude...the snowball effect...

So, what is the possible future of the tourist industry?

There are three categories of leisure travel, of tourism: local, for those who stay close to home, outgoing, for those who travel some distance away, and incoming, for those who come from some distance away...

Locally, or close enough for the vacationers do it by themselves, by car, by train, or even by bicycle, cycling holidays, we will see an increase of so-called popular travel. Some will be visiting their parents or grandparents, their brothers, their sisters, their cousins, or some good old friends. Some will go camping, some others will book a room in an out-of-the-beaten-track family hotel. Those with a larger family, with two or three kids, might opt for a self catering cottage, very much like the average working family did in the aftermath of WWII in Europe, until the 1970's.

Vacationing locally will have a major advantage: people will be aware of the salubrity, of the healthfulness of the area! If the nearby places they wish to visit are open, this will mean that they're safe. No government in their own mind would open unsafe regions just for the sake of getting visitors so the local businesses don't go under...

This being said...

It is clear that different people are telling different stories. While the authorities are trying to avoid a complete collapse of the economy, the health authorities keep repeating loud and clear that the virus is still present and that one must exert a lot of caution…

Clearly, using simple common sense, the people concerned will decide for themselves whether and where, to go or not to go.

On the other hand, outgoing travel will depend on whether the borders are opened or closed: will their own authorities, at home, let them travel to where they want to go? Will airplanes be available? Are they going to be safe? Next question: are the authorities where they'd like to go going to let them in? Is their destination safe? Are the local authorities over there trustworthy? Are the tourist facilities, the sights, the hotels, the restaurants, working and safe?

Many questions indeed, and each and every one of them will generate both, doubts and anxiety…

…and once again, this is not what people are looking for when they go on vacation… especially if their life and that of their family and friends is at stake!

Your conclusion is as good as mine!

No matter what, in the future, at least in the near future, outgoing travel will become rare and therefore expensive. Only those with higher means will be able to afford long distance travel, exotic destinations, very much like in the old days, in the 1800's and at the start of the 1900's, prior to the Great Depression, and prior to the globalization of mass consumption...

Interestingly, in those long gone days, tropical fevers and other nasty bugs were quite frequent, all sorts of deadly diseases for which there were no cures... On the other hand, at the time, apart from a handful of adventurers in search of the Lost Ark, very few people traveled far and wide... The vast majority stayed home or close to home!

Incoming travelers will clearly be in the same situation. In short, does their country allow them to go where they want? Are the destinations where they'd like to go going to accept them, and under which conditions? Many governments have barred travelers from many countries that are judged unsafe...

Due to the travel restrictions and the anxiety caused by the uncertainty of the situation, but also for costs reasons, there will be fewer incoming travelers.

As for the groups, if any at all, they will be small. They will have to be, to fit safely in a bus. As a consequence, the very few bus tours if any at all that might be running will be terribly expensive.

Anyone thinking it's ever going to be like "before" is making a huge mistake!

For their part, the international travelers who will insist on making their own arrangements, if legally possible at all, booking their own flights, and then, at destination, their trains or rented cars, their hotels, etc, these travelers will bump into the local crowds, those who stayed at home or close to home.

They might find the various places somewhat crowded, but also possibly inhospitable, due to the uncertainty of the health situation in parts of the country where they're from... It could be just rumors for that matter, what people hear on the radio or see on TV, or what goes around on the net...

There are so many fake news stories, and everything will have an incidence.

In the end, and no matter what, prices will go up! In other words, there will be fewer visitors from abroad, and not just for health reasons.

More than before, prices will be a determining factor.

We are talking about what had become an industry, the travel industry, but how and when did it start? As often, people tend to forget...

The first paid holidays... Just think, paid holidays! ...companies, corporations paying their employees not to work! What a totally crazy concept for any employer!

In any case, the first paid holidays were introduced in Germany in the second half of the 1800's, for a select few, a handful of white collars. Still in Germany, in the early 1900's, some workers in the brewing industry received three days of paid holidays after one year of employment.

In 1910, the Austro-Hungarian Empire introduced the concept. This was followed by most other European countries after WWI, from the 1920's onward. France and Belgium were the last two, in 1936, right after the Great Depression and just before WWII.

Clearly, at the start, these paid holidays were fairly short, just a few days, and only a few people were concerned.

Following the damage caused by WWII, the necessity to reconstruct Europe and restore the economy forced both, the governments and the employers to introduce more social policies.

The huge losses of population during WWI already had led to the introduction of paid vacations shortly after the war, on a small scale though. For the same reason, and because the work force had become too scarce to risk clashes and industrial action, the same governments and employers were forced to give in to some of the workers' pre-war demands, shorter work week, higher pay, health protection, retirement scheme, and paid holidays…

In the 1930's, following the Great Depression, Europe was in a state of insurrection. Several countries saw the election of Socialist or even Communist governments, which in part led to WWII, but also to the Civil War in Spain…

So, among other benefits, more vacation time was given to the workers, on top of weekends and bank holidays… Weekends… In most places, before WWII, the work week was six days, Monday to Saturday, and if the boss said so, they also worked on Sunday, or else, they were sacked! Jobs were scarce in those days…

Depending on the arrangements negotiated country by country, some got more than others, resulting in what we observe today: two weeks of paid holidays in some countries, up to five weeks or more in others… In the US, they're not a legal obligation; they're left to the employers' discretion and so, some workers don't get any!

In post-WWII Europe, in the late 1940's and in the 1950's, for the city dwellers who lived in an apartment, usually tiny and uncomfortable, paid vacations were something to look forward to, insofar as they could relax and rest, take a break, go somewhere and change their daily routine...

In the mid-1800s, along with the Industrial Revolution, the bourgeoisie, the well-to-do started going to the sea. Sea baths were recommended by the medical profession, and they suddenly became fashionable. Many sea resorts, both in the UK and on the continent remind us of those days. The first ones were fairly close to the main cities: Brighton in England is a short hop from London, while Deauville in France is not too far from Paris, etc... To accommodate the sea baths goers, on top of the sumptuous villas that invaded the seafront, hotels, restaurants, theatres, and gambling casinos were built. They're still there!

Those who lived too far from the sea went to spas instead, *Baden* in German. In Germany and Austria, the cities whose name contains the word Baden are ancient Roman baths. They were always favored by the nobles and the well-to-do, and they became even trendier in the 1800's. Same for Bath in England and Aix-les-Bains in France, among many others!

In the spring and in the fall, when it was too cold to go to the coast, the rich used to travel inland. They either went to the hot springs and to the spas, or else, weather permitting, they took river cruises, on the Rhine, the Main, and the Danube, past the medieval castles, along the hillside vineyards, romantic cruises. A big difference with modern cruises though, they only travelled on the boat, they didn't sleep on it. At night, they stayed in luxury hotels and in castles where they also dined. They usually spent several days at each place, where they visited the surroundings, went wine-tasting, or, for some, connected with distant relatives…

With the development of rail travel, in the mid-1800's, these same well-to-do started traveling further away, like Queen Victoria and the Russian Imperial family who went to Nice on the French Riviera every winter.

As a result, the first thing the workers did when they got their paid holidays was of course to imitate those privileged few. The introduction of mass-consumption which was generalized throughout Europe and the rest of the western world after WWII did the rest!

As automobiles were made available to the workers in Europe in the 50's, they drove to the same places the rich went to before the war. It was the birth of the summer holidays. In some countries, everyone was off for a whole month, either July or August, like it or not!

This had two consequences: first, the development of the leisure infrastructure, hotels, restaurants, gambling casinos, and the roads of course, which soon became toll roads.

Then, as they had been chased away from their former spots, the rich started traveling to far-off destinations. They were able to do so thanks to the post-war modernization of the airplane industry, first, the transformation of freight war planes into passenger planes, then the introduction of new types of airplanes, equipped with reactors instead of propellers, smaller ones at first, the private jets, for a select few and, as time went by, by larger ones, the jumbo jets.

With the birth of charter flights, in the late 60's, early 70's, the less affluent were also able to travel to faraway destinations, like the well-to-do, but not in the same conditions, not first class, and definitely not to the same five star hotels and palaces...

In the same manner as in Europe in the 1800's and the 1900's, the progressive extension of leisure travel to destinations further and further away triggered waves of infrastructure development, along the coast mostly.

From the early sea resorts on either side of the English Channel, it moved first to the French Riviera, Cannes, Nice, Monaco, etc... then to the former colonies, English and French, the Caribbean Islands, the Bahamas, then Cuba, nearby Florida, then it snowballed...

Interestingly, back in the day, the rich travelled to these exotic places during the winter, when the temperatures were mild, at least not so hot... They initiated the snowbird trend, but then it changed! Suddenly, having a suntan became fashionable: it was the proof that one could afford taking a holiday, some sort of bragging out loud!

Little by little, every single spot on any coast anywhere in the world became a potential destination. Those with a large beach and where an airport could be built gained immediate fame, Acapulco, Rio... Florida of course, Hawaii, but also the entire Spanish Mediterranean coast, the Costa del Sol and the Costa Brava, and every place in between... The wealthy people who owned a yacht could also travel around the Mediterranean, go to Capri or the Greek Isles... the precursors of the modern cruises!

All of this is outgoing tourism: the Westerners, in the beginning mostly the Europeans, going somewhere in the world.

At the start, in the 1800's, in industrial Europe, more or less modern-day Western Europe, the select few who were able to travel to exotic destinations did so in grand style. You should read some Agatha Christies' novels for a taste of the opulence of the days, ultimate luxury at every step! In this regard, the movies with Sir Peter Ustinov as Hercule Poirot are absolutely brilliant!

Then, little by little, in addition to the top notch destinations reserved for the rich and famous, affordable vacations were developed for the people with lower income, the workers, the middle class and the lower middle class.

The concept of the vacation village was born.

It started in Europe with nature enthusiasts and campers, in the aftermath of WWII, in the late 40's, early 50's. With time, some became ClubMed or similar, providing accommodation either in bungalow style villages, with palapa roofs, or in hotels, two to five stars...

On the less expensive side, some of the early campsites were turned into real villages, not with tents any more, but mobile homes, sometimes hundreds of them, with swimming pools, stores, restaurants, and even entertainment...

The all-inclusive resorts, all of them, all over the world, owe their existence to the same ClubMed concept! In a way, the extra large cruise ships as well!

There are also the more individual holidaymakers, those who drive around with their caravans or their motor homes, a few days here, and a few days there. They usually congregate on dedicated sites which provide running water and electricity... In the end, it's just another form of the same thing!

Of course, these concepts eventually spread to the whole of Europe, north and south, east and west, then North America, Australia, New Zealand, etc...

Little by little, the entire world got into a traveling mood. Well, those who could afford it that is, still just a handful!

In order to boost their income, the various organizers decided to widen the base of the pyramid, to increase their market by making the product more accessible!

Mass travel was born.

Again, like the automobile at the start, it implied quality affordable products. Flying became cheaper and airplanes bigger. Hotels became bigger, and prices lower... always bigger in order to be cheaper!

It's the fast food principle.

There are many more poor people than rich people in the world so, if you sell a product at a lower than low price, you gain access to a much wider market, and if you do it well, you increase your market share. As it says, small streams make big rivers, and so, you multiply your tiny per-customer profit exponentially, as long as what you sell, and this is of paramount importance, as long as what you sell has a good value-for-money ratio!

This is where a lot of self proclaimed tour operators made mistakes and went bust, and not just tour operators for that matter. The same happened in every other business field!

Fast bucks and cheap profit, in short, greed...

And so, naturally, this brings us to the low-cost cruises, the last link in a long chain of constantly more affordable vacations.

If you're looking to make things always cheaper, you know that, past a certain point, you can't expect a quality product anymore. There is a limit below which it is financially impossible to go. It's called the breakeven point! No matter what, in order to maintain an acceptable quality, someone at some point has to pay! Of course, there are ways to go about this.

One in particular has been used for some time; let's call it the airplane principle.

Modern airplanes offer a lot of inexpensive seats, the cheaper they are and the fuller the plane will be, in theory. Very little profit is made on them if any. They normally cover the operating costs, the fuel, the maintenance, the crew, etc… If the planes aren't fully booked for too long a time, the airlines can go bankrupt.

So, to make up for the lack of income on the economy seats, the airlines also offer first class seats, the famous front cabin. This is where they make their profit…

Well, it's the same on a cruise ship!

Apart from a few luxury cabins, the only things that glitter are the cover of the brochure and the TV ads, and also the public parts of the ship of course, the huge chandeliers in the foyer, and the thousand and one lights.

As for the cabins, they range from two star hotel, for the smaller ones, to five star hotel for the suites. To sell the cheaper cabins, the travel agents tell their customers that they will only use them for sleeping, and that while they're asleep, the size is irrelevant! It's a sales technique, and it works! With this kind of approach, they have managed to fill enormous cruise ships with many different nationalities...

Here as well, there are a few helpful tricks of course, wide-angle photography for one: it makes a small cabin appear much bigger than it is. Cheap hotels do the same thing! In addition, the brochures often use pictures of the larger cabins, or even of the suites, to make people fantasize and hook them!

The price of a cabin doesn't entirely rest on its size either: the location matters greatly, the higher the deck, the dearer. It also depends on whether they have a view or not! Some cabins have a private balcony with a sea view. Usually, the higher the deck, the larger the balcony, and the higher the price of course!

The rule is extremely simple: the more expensive, the more expensive...

It's easier to add a few bucks to the price when it's already high! On the other hand, adding a couple of bucks on the cheaper cabins could mean that the clients will travel with someone else!

To justify the huge price difference that first class passengers are charged, they get extra personal service... Yes, sometimes they dine at the table of the Captain, it's part of the package!

On a plane, in the front cabin, they get better seats, better food, better drinks, altogether, much better service... they also pay five or six times, sometimes up to ten times the price of an economy ticket! They sure could buy a few romantic dinners in a classy restaurant for the same money!

These high prices are the main reason why the first class is mostly used for corporate travel and not by vacationers, unless they've earned a lot of frequent flyer miles on business trips...

Getting back to the cruise, whether the passengers travel economy or first class, there are extra costs, and they're well advertized: the famous optional excursions.

To see the few sights, when the ship stops, usually in the morning after a whole night at sea, the passengers have to pay extra. These optional excursions are an important source of revenue for the cruise operators. In addition, while the passengers are ashore, the staff has the time to clean the ship and make the rooms!

At the beginning, in the days of Hercule Poirot, the ships called in at ports where they got coal for the engines, filled the drinking water tanks, and replenished the cold chambers with block ice to keep them cool until the next stop. They also got fresh food for a few days.

While this was taken care of, those who didn't feel well enough to go to shore stayed on the ship and took advantage of the onboard facilities, the bar and the restaurant, or they relaxed on the deck. The others got off and tried the local specialties, like the bouillabaisse in Marseille for instance!

As for the more adventurous, they hired taxis or whatever else was available, horse carriages or even camels in Egypt, and they went to visit the local sights. This eventually became the optional sightseeing excursion, nowadays organized and sold by the cruise operators...

At the time of Hercule Poirot, cruise-goers were not in a hurry. The ship stopped for several days, two at the very least. Nowadays, time is limited, the visits are rushed, so much so that sometimes the passengers barely know where they are! Worse, if the ship carries 5,000 or 6,000 passengers, the number of buses going to the same place at the same time can be grotesque... people can easily forget which bus they're on. It may happen that they miss the return transfer, or even the departure of the ship. I hear this is quite frequent in places like Monte Carlo where it's so easy to get lost!

Wherever these modern extra large cruise ships call, you can see the passengers who go on the excursions follow their local host, or rather, their little signs, red, blue, green, or yellow, with a letter A, B, C... They're just being herded there and back... "No time to stop, no time to shop, hurry, hurry, the others are right behind..."

Relaxing holidays?

As for the people at the ports of call, the locals, they mostly complain that the passengers are like the cruise, they're cheap! They don't buy a thing. If anything at all, they complain it's too expensive! They even carry their own plastic bottle of water, which they usually leave behind, creating more pollution, 5,000 people, 5,000 bottles, multiplied by so many ships a day... nearly every day!

Same thing for the meals which they take on the ship, they're included! And so, apart from the cruise operators who seem to be the only ones making money, and the passengers hopefully having a good time, what good are the low-cost cruises?

They create chaos from the moment the passengers get off the ship to go and see the local sights. As for the ships, they are responsible for some of the worst air pollution as they burn the filthiest fuel, even when they're docked, waiting for the passengers to return from the optional excursions.

In addition, if, back in the day, they used to buy supplies when they stopped, they don't anymore. They restock the ship before the start of the cruise. They fill the refrigerators and the freezers for several weeks if necessary.

To say the least, people have become weary of these extra large cruise ships...

Ask the locals in Venice!

Mass tourism has grown in the footsteps of the rich and famous of the Romantic Era, in the nineteenth century, but in those days, people traveled in style. They supported the local economy wherever they went. As a matter of fact, the tour buses still do. Wherever they go, they use the hotels, the restaurants, and the shops, etc…

On the other hand, the modern travelers are almost always either on a shoe string or on an all-inclusive, on a cheap cruise or on a super budget vacation.

Florence, in Italy, recently passed a law prohibiting the tourists from sitting on a curb or on the steps of a church. Italians eat and drink in a restaurant, or at home; they sit at a table, not on the ground… Many popular sites throughout Europe have introduced similar restrictions in order to limit the negative impact of low-cost travelers.

As a matter of fact, Florence is only the tip of the iceberg. Many people all over the world would rather not see them at all! They have no positive influence on the local economy whatsoever. They rarely if ever support the hotels, the restaurants, or even the shops, apart from the minimarts or the fast-food places where they get their sandwiches and their sodas, before dumping the empty bags and the plastic packaging on the street…

Low-cost travel is not something new. It started with charter flights back in the 1970's. What is new though is the numbers, the masses of people going to the same place at the same time.

Like Florence and Venice, many destinations all over the world have suffered from the ever increasing overflow of low-cost mass tourism ...

November 1991 did not cause the crisis, far from it, but for many visitors who used to come to Europe every year, every two years, it was the coup de grace, the last straw...

From then on, one had to fight to walk across Saint Mark's Square, to jostle for space everywhere they went in Europe, like in the subway at rush-hour.

When the wall between Eastern and Western Europe came down, people from the East got on whatever buses they could find, usually in pretty bad shape, and they took off. Don't get me wrong, nobody blames them for wanting to see what they had been deprived of for so long!

The East European currencies were worth nothing on the other side of the wall so, before they left, they filled their trunks with food and drinks. Then, they headed for the famous sites, mainly Italy. Most of them wanted to go to Rome, because of the Polish Pope, John Paul II...

Even if most groups had two or three drivers, they still had to stop along the way... They got on the toll roads but they couldn't pay; they'd get to the toll gate and say they had no money, which was usually true, and they'd let them through. When they reached their destination, they stopped on the cark parks, for a day or two. They couldn't pay them either!

After a while, the authorities made it mandatory for buses to pay for city parking before entering. In addition, the car parks were equipped with low steel bars to prevent buses from going in, all over Europe, because this went on everywhere!

In Venice, the poor things couldn't pay for the public boat, the vaporetto, so they walked from the Tronchetto bus parking to Saint Mark Square, a long, long way. Later on, they walked back to the bus, to grab some food out of the trunk... and they returned to St. Mark's Square once again. All they did was walk back and forth between the bus and the square.

At night, they couldn't afford to stay in a hotel, so they slept on the bus. The next morning, they used the facilities on the parking, the restrooms and the showers normally reserved for the bus drivers. Everything was quickly soiled and out of order...

Then the shop keepers around Saint Mark's square started complaining about the penniless crowds. They walked around the square all day long, clockwise, counterclockwise; they had nowhere else to go, nothing else to do...

At some point, there were so many of them that they drove away the few tourists who still supported the hotels, the restaurants and the shops, the older generation middleclass westerners.

They left and never came back.

In actual fact, the real reason for their disaffection was financial, but everything collided, one problem added to the other. Not only did the financial crises, one after the other, plunge them into disarray, but all of a sudden, the places they used to go to, to change their mind and relax, the places they had enjoyed for many years were not enjoyable any longer...

Gradually but irremediably, the western middleclass lost its financial might. Due to the successive collapses of both, the economy and the stock market, those who once were the core of the high spending travelers suddenly lost their means; some lost their pension and even had to get a job to survive...

Those who made it through the financial crises without too much damage changed their habits. They stayed away from the hustle and bustle, from the madness Europe had become, and they started traveling on cruise ships, more relaxing, less hassle...

The cruise ship trend started with the fall of the wall, in the early 1990's. In the beginning, the ships were older and smaller, but as the numbers increased, so did their size…

And so, a new generation of low-cost clientele emerged.

At the start, they traveled the same way as their predecessors, but it couldn't last long without the proper means. That's why and when the European bus tours lost their appeal. Due to the new safety regulations, the prices went up which totally discouraged them.

So, for the younger ones mostly, they arranged their trips through the internet, thanks to the booking platforms for both, the hotels and the airlines. As for the older ones, they went on low-cost cruises… By then, the ships were already quite big!

Little by little, from the early 90's, for lack of income, but also because they were getting older, people stopped traveling the way their parents and grandparents did back in the 60's and the 70's. Suddenly, the spirit of "If it's Tuesday this must be Belgium" disappeared.

The people who were most impacted by the successive financial crises not only stopped traveling but they stopped supporting the consumer society as a whole. This was happening long before the Coronavirus. Now, it just got a lot worse!

Getting more visitors from overseas has always been the biggest difficulty for the various tourist destinations throughout the world. This went on until charter flights became available, in the late 60's, early 70's, when air travel became more affordable. Then the major airlines lowered their prices, and finally, the low-cost airlines appeared, with a major difference in terms of onboard service though: people didn't travel anymore, they were merely transported... everything else cost extra!

The end of WWII saw the first guided bus tours. They were organized for the soldiers of the Allied Forces stationed in and around London. They went on a day trip to Stratford upon Avon or to Stonehenge. Some went to Canterbury, to visit the Cathedral. A few carried on to the English coast, to the White Cliffs of Dover. From there, on a clear day, they could see the coast of France...

Very much the same happened in Switzerland. At the end of the war, they offered trips to the Italian Lakes, to Milan, Venice or Florence, and even to Rome, for the religious groups...

That's for the incoming tourism, until the fall of the wall and the concomitant collapse of the economy. This in turn led to both, the rise of mass-travel and the downfall of quality touring... From then on, it just went down, irremediably, and fast.

As it says, nature abhors a vacuum...

So, a few things happened.

First, the so-called Eastern Divisions of the main tour operators did all they could to compensate the loss of the middle class western travelers. They had hotel beds to fill. Both the Chinese and the Indians did that, but at the beginning, their buying power was fairly low. So, very soon, their numbers made up for their lack of individual spending capacity, hence the crowds they quickly became.

Unfortunately, some not so clever greedy local operators played dirty tricks on them. As a result, both the Chinese and the Indians started running their own operations, the restaurants at first, then everything else. They contracted incoming tour operators owned by some of their immigrated nationals. If there weren't any, they simply created them, mostly the Chinese for that matter; very clever business people indeed.

The Europeans shot themselves in the foot. Very silly to say the least! The Asian tourists ended up coming by the hundreds of thousands and more.

They not only brought the groups, but they also ran the various businesses and of course, they kept the profits.

Back in the early 70's, the first few Japanese people arrived in Europe, rarely more than three or four at a time. They were taking pictures of everything, mostly shop windows, display windows... The rumor had it, it was merely industrial spying!

A little later, towards the end of the 70's, the real Japanese tourists started coming. Their numbers greatly increased in the 80's, and then, they suddenly declined, also as a result of the successive financial crises and the subsequent downfall of the economy.

Meanwhile, the west, North America, Australia, New Zealand and Europe had relocated much of their industrial activity to China and India. So, putting two and two together...

In 2019, there were very few Japanese tourists in Europe, but masses of Chinese and Indians. You couldn't go anywhere without running into throngs of them.

Meanwhile in the west…

In the early 90's, a few entrepreneurs came up with global alternatives, this time for the westerners…

To compensate for their loss of revenue, some land tour operators invested in cruise ships. They either had them built or they acquired existing cruise companies, mostly river cruises. A few international ocean cruise companies invested in river cruises as well. The competition became fierce, and the traffic on the European rivers, the Seine, the Rhine, the Rhone, the Danube and a few others, increased exponentially…

For their part, the ocean cruise lines that didn't get into the river cruise business started building much larger ships, always larger: the more people, the cheaper the cruise, the cheaper the cruise, the more people… until the winter 2019/2020…

Ten thousand passengers and crew on the same ship, with rumors of even larger vessels… Not surprising that the locals didn't like them!

In many areas where they used to call, the coast has been damaged beyond recovery, the corals have died, the sea bottom is covered with litter, plastic bottles and bags, aluminum containers…

Even the cheap souvenir shops were unhappy! Too many people at the same time, not enough time to stop and shop, and usually, not one client with money to spend... They were not only rushed, but they were also broke, and mingy! Low-cost cruises with passengers who were on a budget already before they went on the cruise!

I was watching these tour buses in Valladolid, in touristy Yucatan, fifteen, twenty 14 meter buses, all pulling in at more or less the same time, every morning, doing the same day excursion, from the overcrowded Costa Maya to the nearby archeological sites. They'd arrive in Valladolid and stop for thirty minutes, just for the sake of saying they'd stopped there, merely adding a name on the description of the excursion, so it looked better and it justified the price... cosmetics!

It was not a toilet stop, they have onboard facilities! It was not a coffee break either, they'd just had their breakfast, and there's no place to get a proper cup of coffee, just this nasty instant coffee...

The passengers had nowhere to go, nor any time to do anything... As a matter of fact, there is not much to do in half an hour in the center of Valladolid, apart from a rushed visit to the Cathedral, but even that was not included!

More buses came in the afternoon, after a hurried visit to Chichen Itza. Same thing, even worse, by then, it was hot, really hot, and the people were dead exhausted! All they wanted to do was go back to their hotel and jump in the pool!

The all inclusive week on the Costa Maya, a long cocktail party by the pool, with a couple of friends, Margarita and Pina Colada...

In Valladolid, Yucatan, most of the groups looked as if they were on a low-cost cruise. In fact, many of these all-inclusive Costa Maya trips are even cheaper than cheap cruises! The few shopkeepers around the main square in Valladolid didn't try to sell them anything, not even a T-shirt!

As for the guides and the bus drivers, they made a living doing the same trip over and over again, day after day. They had a job, but they were largely underpaid.

Low-cost cruises, low-cost all-inclusive, including the trip to Chichen Itza!

Since the 60's and the 70's, tourism as an industry has transformed the global economy, hotels, restaurants, trains, buses and airplanes, even the banking system, with the Travelers' Checks at first, then the credit cards and the money transfer companies.

So many activities are connected to tourism, and so many people depend on it for their income, directly or indirectly. So when tourism stops, the whole world stops.

Strangely enough, some politicians seem not to grasp the importance of tourism. They talk about the automobile industry, about the airplane industry and about construction, but they seem to miss the bigger picture!

Without a job, those who normally work in tourism aren't going to get a new car, they're not going to take a plane or even a bus or a train to some relaxing destination after a long and arduous season, and they're most definitely not going to buy a new home...

The snowball effect...

Providing them with a job ought to be a priority. This would be solved by re-starting the economy as a whole, beginning with the service providers, the restaurants, the hotels, the transport companies, etc...

Yes, it's easier said than done!

Due to the new health regulations which must be implemented for fear of an explosion of the pandemic, the infamous second wave everyone talks about, tourism will never be the same.

Mass and numbers belong to the past. The volumes we have known will never be seen again. This means that both, the transport industry, planes, buses, and trains, and the infrastructure industry, hotels, restaurants, etc… will suffer a serious blow, fatal for some.

As a consequence, many of those who worked in those industries will lose their job, some already have, and without a job, they're not going to consume!

The snowball effect…

Always getting back to mass consumption, always more, of everything, of anything, and always cheaper, to get more and more consumers…

When I was a kid, traveling was rare and costly, like books. Then, cheap pocket books became available, mass produced at a lower cost, sold at a reduced price. And then the internet came up…

Same for vacations! Travel agencies opened outlets in the shopping malls, between the fast food giant and the discount supermarket. The once-in-alifetime trip of the 60's and the 70's became the same as a hamburger or a box of genetically modified breakfast cereals... And once again the internet came up...

In the last few years in Europe, online booking and low-cost airlines made it possible to go to Amsterdam, Barcelona, Rome or Venice for the weekend, for next to nothing. There were so many planes up in the sky that sunsets were marred by their contrails, not to mention the induced pollution...

Mass tourism...

It's the same on the roads of course. Two or three tour buses a day on the average between Lucerne, Switzerland and Innsbruck, Austria, back in the mid-70's, until well over fifty just a few months ago, all travelling on the freeways, bumper to bumper...

And it was ten times worse in Italy, between Venice, Florence, and Rome... a nightmare.

Watch that movie, "If it's Tuesday..." This is what a tour of Europe looked like in the late 60's, great fun indeed, as opposed to the industrial trips that they ran until a few months ago! It is not surprising that people didn't book bus tours anymore; it is not surprising that they switched to cruises...

Well, it's all finished for now!

Clearly, this pandemic will be a life changer. It might help correct the excesses brought in by unrestrained consumerism…

Printed in Great Britain
by Amazon

57841346R00088